Patriotism and Honor: Veterans of Dutchess County, New York

Part II

Dutchess County Historical Society
2019 Yearbook • Volume 98

Candace J. Lewis, *Editor*

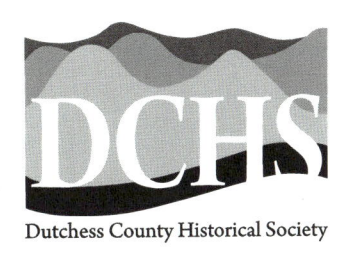

Dutchess County Historical Society

The Dutchess County Historical Society is a not-for-profit educational organization that collects, preserves, and interprets the history of Dutchess County, New York, from the period of the arrival of the first Native Americans until the present day.

Publications Committee:

Candace J. Lewis, Ph.D., *Editor*
David Dengel, Dennis Dengel, John Desmond,
Roger Donway, Eileen Hayden,
Bill Jeffway, Melodye Moore,
and William P. Tatum III Ph.D.

Designer: Marla Neville, Main Printing, Poughkeepsie, New York
mymainprinter.com

Printer: Elizabeth Lewis, Advertisers Printing Co., Saint Louis, MO
elewis@advprinting.com

Dutchess County Historical Society Yearbook 2019
Volume 98 • Published annually since 1915
Copyright © by Dutchess County Historical Society
ISSN: 0739-8565
ISBN: 978-0-944733-14-1

Cover: Top: Young men of Dutchess County recently transformed into sailors. On the steps of the Armory, Poughkeepsie, New York. 1917. Detail. All Photographs by Reuben P. Van Vlack. Collection of the Dutchess County Historical Society. Bottom: September 20, 1917, the second of six draft contingents in 1917 are escorted to the Poughkeepsie train station. In this instance, the largest of the six, Governor Whitman attends. Functioning as a means to gather coins and bills for a "smokes fund" for the soldiers, the first flag is carried by the local Elks Lodge (B.P.O.E), earning $271. The second flag is carried by employees of the Prudential Company, earning $46.

Back Cover: African-American draftees walking with suitcases to "entrain" from Poughkeepsie station for service. Recruitment of persons of color was segregated. They no doubt wished to serve their country with honor and pride in anticipation of better days ahead. 1917.

The Dutchess County Historical Society Yearbook does not assume responsibility for statements of fact or opinion made by the authors.

Dutchess County Historical Society
P.O. Box 88
Poughkeepsie, NY 12602
845-471-1630
email: contact@dchsny.org
dchsny.org

This issue of the Dutchesss County Historical Society's yearbook has been generously underwritten by the following:

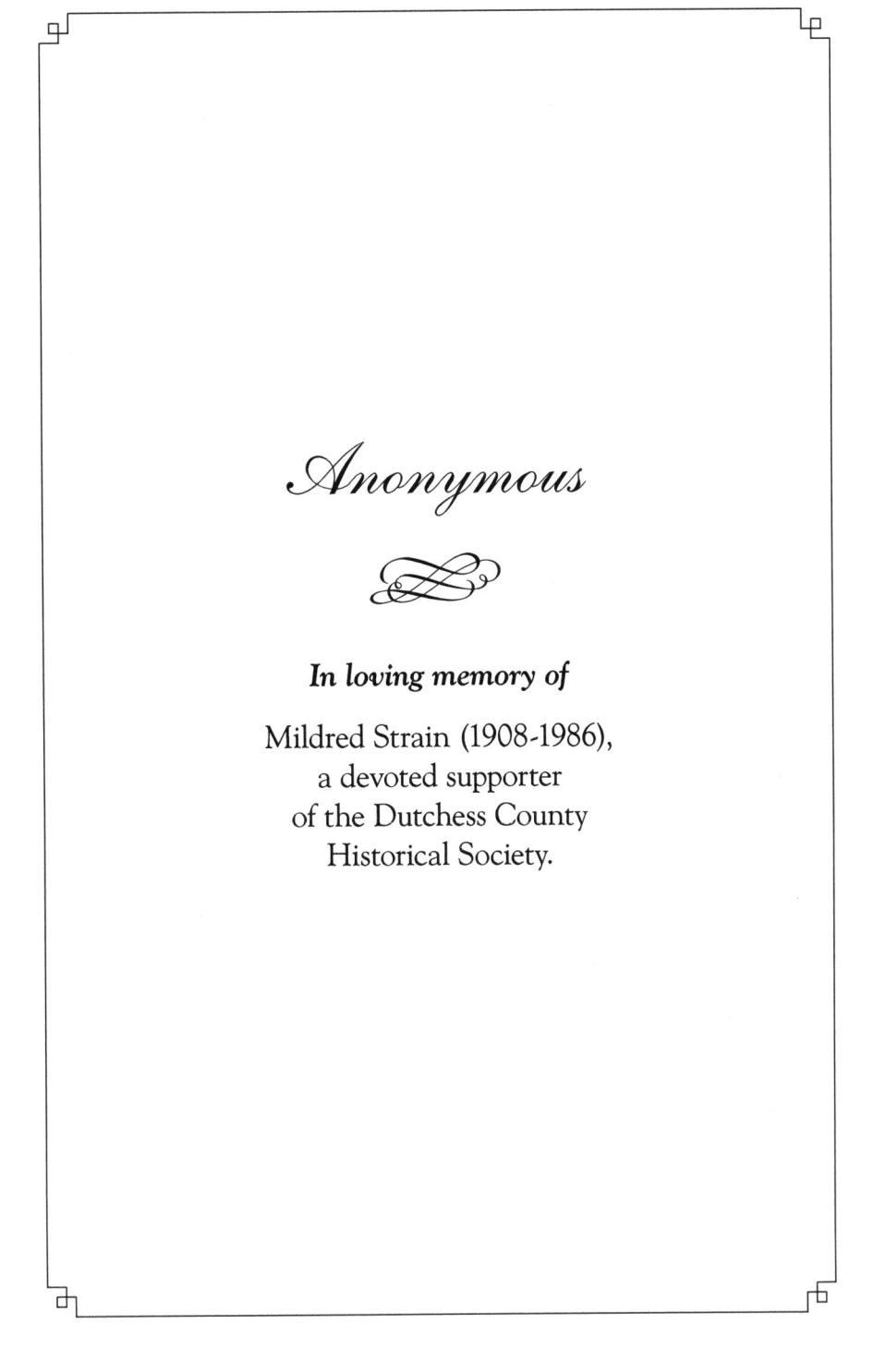

Anonymous

In loving memory of

Mildred Strain (1908-1986),
a devoted supporter
of the Dutchess County
Historical Society.

Anonymous

Joan Smith

In loving memory of
James R. Smith (1946-2016)

Shirley M. Handel

LTC Gilbert A. Krom

In memory of a beloved brother
and fine soldier.

David Dengel
Dennis Dengel

We support our men and women in uniform.

Lou and Candace J. Lewis

F. Julius and Carla Gude

Eileen Mylod Hayden

and

Dr. Benjamin Hayden

Poughkeepsie Public Library District
is proud of its longtime association with the Dutchess County Historical Society. Together we offer our community a selection of exciting avenues into our fascinating past.

ZIMMER BROTHERS
JEWELERS SINCE 1893

ZB DESIGN CENTER
Design Inspired By You

visit us in Poughkeepsie and Rhinebeck

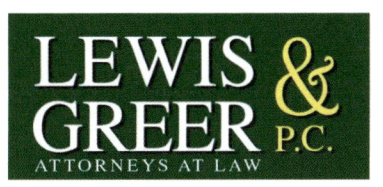

LEWIS & GREER P.C.
ATTORNEYS AT LAW

Corporate, Commercial
& Business Law;
Construction Law;
Municipal Law;
Real Property Tax Law

Lou Lewis

J. Scott Greer

~

Dylan C. Harris

Phil Giamportone

510 Haight Avenue, Suite 202 • Poughkeepsie, NY 12603
Phone: (845) 454-1200 • Fax (845) 454-3315
Visit our website at www.**lewisgreer.com**

Lights, Camera - Auction!

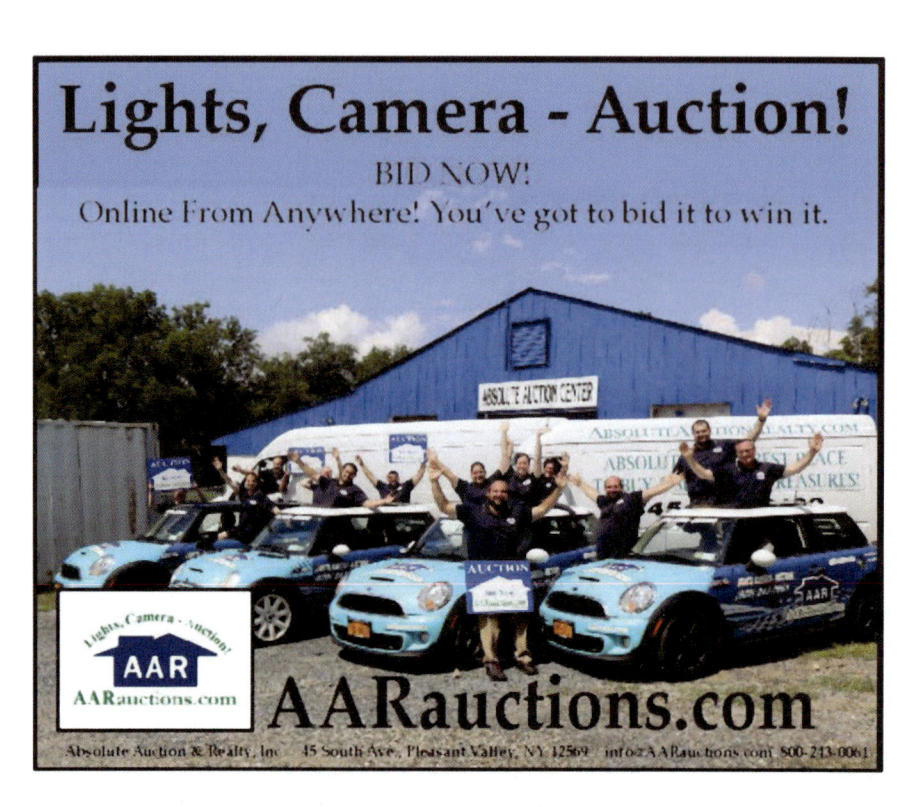

BID NOW!
Online From Anywhere! You've got to bid it to win it.

AARauctions.com

Absolute Auction & Realty, Inc. 45 South Ave., Pleasant Valley, NY 12569 info@AARauctions.com 800-243-0061

D'Arcangelo & Co., LLP
CERTIFIED PUBLIC ACCOUNTANTS & CONSULTANTS

Powered by excellence,
Proven by results.

www.darcangelo.com   Poughkeepsie | Millbrook

TAX SERVICES - ESTATES & TRUSTS - VALUATIONS
AUDITING & ASSURANCE - BUSINESS CONSULTING

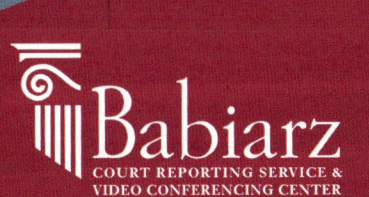

- Court Reporting
- Video Conferencing
- Audio Transcription
- Litigation Support

www.babiarzreporting.com

Raising the Bar
ON LEGAL & BUSINESS REPORTING

Babiarz
COURT REPORTING SERVICE &
VIDEO CONFERENCING CENTER

845-471-2511
Poughkeepsie, NY

866-282-0671
White Plains, NY &
Nyack, NY

845-565-1801
Newburgh, NY

Lillian Loomis, *Poughkeepsie Rooftops*. N.d. Woodcut.

Collection of Eileen Mylod Hayden. Although this print is not dated, we can place it in the decade of the 1930s, after the formation of the Barrett Art Association to which the artist belonged and the construction of the Mid-Hudson Bridge (1929-1930) shown in the image. The view may have represented a vantage point from the Former Amrita Club, including well known buildings such as the Orthodox Jewish Synagogue. On the other hand, the view may be partially imaginary.

In Memoriam

Julia Hotton

Member of the
Dutchess County Historical Society
Board of Trustees

We are sad to report the passing of Julia Hotton on August 5, 2019. She was a valued member of the Board of Trustees at the Dutchess County Historical Society for over six years and a member of the organization for many years before her service on the board. She wrote and published two articles for the DCHS Yearbook (in 2014 and 2017).

Ms. Hotton was the former Assistant Director, responsible for education, at the Brooklyn Museum. She was retired from the New York Public Library Schomburg Center for Research in Black Culture as curator and manager of its Art and Artifacts collection, and there she also directed educational and cultural programs in African American history.

As an independent curator, Ms. Hotton organized a variety of art and historical exhibitions for the New York Historical Society, the Mariners Museum in Newport News Virginia, Syracuse University, and Manhattan East Gallery of Fine Arts. She is survived by her daughter Tanya.

Table of Contents

Letter from the Editor *Candace J. Lewis* xix

Call for Articles: Yearbook 2020 xxi

2019: The Year in Review *by Bill Jeffway* xxiii

FORUM: Patriotism and Honor:
Veterans of Dutchess County, New York, Part II

Lieutenant Alvin H. Treadwell Lost and Found 3
by Peter Bedrossian

Dutchess County's African-American Experience During the World
War, 1917 to 1919…and beyond 9
by Bill Jeffway and Melodye K. Moore

Decoding the Past: George Wuest's First World War Adventures 19
by William P. Tatum III

Immigrant Farmer in the OSS 31
by Julian Strauss

"Orchestrated Hell": Edward R. Murrow's December 1943
radio broadcast, Reporting on his RAF bomber flight over
Nazi Germany 43
by John Barry (commentary),

Bernard Handel's Recollections of World War II 55
by Candace Lewis (ed.)

The Fighting O'Connells: Twentieth Century American Soldiers 63
by Candace Lewis

ARTICLES: Miscellaneous Topics in Dutchess County History

The Clarks of Nagaland 83
by Elizabeth C. Strauss

DCHS Yearbooks Open Windows into
"Invisible" Black Community 99
by Bill Jeffway

Raise High the Roof Beam, Carpenter:
Profile of a Consummate Volunteer 105
by John Desmond

We Three Can Still Hear the Whistle Blowin' 123
by John Desmond

Locusts and Lincoln 133
by Margaret Duff

Let Us Go For an Afternoon Walk Around Hopewell Junction 123
by Charlotte Dodge (1913-2009)

ADDENDA

Contributors 143

DCHS Trustees and Staff 146

DCHS Vice Presidents 147

Municipal Historians and Historical Societies of
Dutchess County 148

Dutchess County Bar Association Celebrates 100 Years 152

DCHS Donors 158

Dutchess County Historical Society Membership 163

Letter from the Editor

He was at the helm in the small hours of the morning. A pea-soup fog had engulfed the ship. He had been in conditions like this dozens of times before, because he had grown up on boats along the New England coast, but now Jack was a first lieutenant in the U.S. Navy, a strapping twenty-five year-old, 6 ft. 4 in.—a tall, a smart, even-tempered fellow.

He was alone at the helm, alone managing the navigating, blind in the concealing weather with everyone asleep below decks, including the captain. And enemy Japanese could be expected to appear at any time. Not only was he concerned about the Japanese, but he did not want to collide with another U.S. Navy ship in the convoy simply because he was blinded by the weather. Radar was in its infancy and not totally to be trusted. He had to make a decision now in the early hours of the morning. He did not want the captain or his crewmates to make fun of him for calling for help, but he was concerned for the safety of the ship. He was not confident in his abilities to handle the ship in the difficult weather conditions with the enemy so near. So he roused a midshipman to go bring the captain to relieve him.

Jack was my father—my step-father—who fought in the Pacific theater in World War II. He told me this story much later when he was ninety years old. It was not a story of intense combat, but of a young man's moment of decision in war. It was a moment that stayed vivid in his memory.

So many American families have stories like this one, brief anecdotes of military service from citizen-soldiers like Jack or professional soldiers who dedicate their careers to the Army, Navy, Marines, Air Force, or Coast Guard. This volume—the second in a series—is devoted to the men and women who give their time and their lives to our country. Because we believe in democracy; we believe in America.

— *Candace J. Lewis, Ph.D., editor*

Call for Articles: Yearbook 2020

Women of Dutchess County, New York: Voices and Talents

Deadline: We are expecting submission of articles by **February 1, 2020**. We look forward with delight to reading your essays

The yearbook is planned to coordinate with the Dutchess County Historical Society's programming also on the topic of "Women of Dutchess: Voices and Talents." In 2020, the central topic for the yearbook will be Dutchess County, New York women throughout our history (up to 50 years ago, our usual limit). Extraordinary women and ordinary women will be the focus of stories, examinations, and essays in our book commemorating the final achievement of the Right to Vote nationwide in the year 1920, one hundred years ago

In 2020, as for the last several years, the yearbook will be divided into sections:

(1) The Forum section will focus on essays and stories about women of Dutchess County. Articles may include topics from the more abstract such as discussions of women within historical movements to quite concrete matters such as accounts of individual residents of the county.

(2) The Articles section will be devoted to essays on any worthwhile research regarding Dutchess County history.

Please submit your article to me in digital form as a Microsoft Word document. Articles for the Forum and Articles sections should be 2,000 to 4,000 words long. If possible, please submit at least one or two images with captions with each essay. Please check for copyright clearance. Send the images separately as jpegs (300 dpi or larger). Images may be black-and-white or color. Please send them with the draft, the figure captions indicated in the text (images are not an afterthought). Copyright will be shared between the Dutchess County Historical Society and the author. The author may re-issue the article in the year after it is published

Continued

in the DCHS yearbook. DCHS asks that we be notified of any republication of your article.

For endnotes, please use *Chicago Manual of Style*. Examples of endnotes:

> Franklin D. Roosevelt, 508th Press Conference, December 10, 1938, *Public Papers and Addresses of Franklin D. Roosevelt, 1938 Volume: The Continuing Struggle for Liberalism* (New York: Macmillan, 1941), 632.
>
> Nancy V. Kelly, "Rhinebeck: Transition in 1799" in *The Hudson Valley Regional Review* Vol. 6, No. 2 (March 1989), 94.

If you have an idea for an article that you are considering, but are doubtful about, just write to me and I will be happy to discuss it.

— Candace Lewis, *Editor*

Review of the Year 2019

*by Bill Jeffway
Executive Director*

We are grateful to all our members, to those who donate time, collections, and/or funding, all of which allow us to continue to rapidly expand our commitment to identify, preserve and share the history of the people of our county. Some summary items of the past year:

Over Here: The Untold Stories of the Men, Women and Children of the World War 1917 to 1919. Well-received installations in Red Hook and Beacon of this traveling exhibition that launched in April 2018 at the FDR Presidential Library & Museum, mean that the exhibition has been to virtually every city and town in the county. It remains available both as a traveling exhibition and permanent online exhibition.

"I served…" From our research on WWI on its centennial, it became painfully clear that stories of veterans and civilians, who serve our country in times of need, too often are not captured, preserved, and shared. As a result, we have successfully piloted and launched the program, "I served…" to begin to capture the stories of living veterans. Enthusiastically endorsed by veterans and veterans' organizations, the future of the program will lie with our ability to secure funding.

Band of Locals. The exhibition, "Band of Locals" at the FDR Presidential Library & Museum looked at the handful of local historians FDR relied on through his adult life in pursuit of his hobby and passion, local history. They happen to be the early founders of DCHS. The spring exhibition was extended through the summer due to public interest.

2020 Focus: Women's Voices & Talents. Foundational work for the upcoming year's theme was begun with the Collections gift of 20 paintings, and an enormous number of sketches, letters, and documents related to the artist from Lagrange, Caroline Morgan Clowes. Nationally recognized in 1876, her legacy as a painter of local landscapes and farm animals, has been allowed to drift unnecessarily into obscurity. As the name of the year's theme suggests, we will be looking at a broad range of talents of women in the county on the 100th anniversary of women gaining the right to vote at a national level.

Significant New Move into Educational Support. Given a $10,000 grant from the National Society Daughters of the American Revolution and its Mahwenawasigh Chapter, as well as a $5,000 Corporate Sponsorship from Central Hudson Gas & Electric, and $10,000 in other fundraising conducted by DCHS, we are creating a permanent, easily-accessible set of videos and discussion guides for High School education levels based on our research on World War One.

Memorial Gifts. We accepted with deep humility and gratitude, Memorial Donations recognizing Walter Patrice and Gaye Kendall, both of whom had a positive and lasting impact on the understanding of, respect for, and enjoyment of, our shared local history.

FORUM

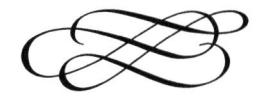

Lieutenant Alvin H. Treadwell Lost and Found

by Peter Bedrossian

The Great War or the World War as World War I was known during the 1920s and 1930s left behind many stories. Often those stories were made by those unknown to the readers and became almost fictional accounts of daring and sacrifice. War though is very democratic and impacts those near and far, known and unknown. This essay is about one who was both local and known in his community. The essay is an outgrowth of a project undertaken for the Centennial of the Great War. I developed an annotated list of those Dutchess County residents whose names appeared in the updated Honor Roll of War dead as published in the *Poughkeepsie Eagle* in 1926.[1] One name that stood out was First Lieutenant Alvin H. Treadwell. It was not his rank but two items which caught my eye: One was his date of death, November 16, 1918: five days after the Armistice. The second item was his unit: the 213th Aero Squadron. He died as a pilot, one of the "Knights of the Air." Treadwell's occupation as a flyer suggested that there was more to learn about this rare breed of the Great War, one of the few from this region.

Son of a Vassar College Professor

Alvin Treadwell, born August 16, 1896, was the son of Aaron Louis Treadwell and Sarah Maria Treadwell. He was raised in Poughkeepsie as his father was a Zoology professor at Vassar College. As a faculty member, Professor Treadwell lived on campus with his family, so it made sense that the address on young Treadwell's New York Army card reads "Vassar College."[2] At first, I was wondering how there was a male college student at Vassar! His father's position clarified the anachronism of a male college-aged student living at Vassar College. He was not a student, simply a member of a faculty family.

The combination of his academic ability, athletic prowess, and his father's status all but guaranteed that young Treadwell would attend college, and likely an Ivy League institution. He initially chose Wesleyan University, but transferred to Yale in 1916 and was a member of the class of 1918. He was likely aware of the progress of the war and most certainly aware that Yale students formed the first Naval Aviation Unit in 1916.[3] It is unknown what influence this may have had on young Treadwell. However, when the Yale unit became popular in the Spring of 1917, there was not enough space in the program to accommodate all those interested and perhaps this contributed to his considering service outside of Yale.

Becoming an Aviator and Leading Combat Missions

Thus, when America declared war on April 5, 1917, Alvin Treadwell did not wait long to act. In May 1917, he left Yale, for Madison Barracks, New York. After three months there, he went to Cornell for a month-long session for aviation ground training. In September 1917, he went to an aviators training camp near Tours, France, as a Cadet Officer. He completed his training and was commissioned a First Lieutenant on March 2, 1918.[4] Two months later, he joined Escadrille 154, a French aviation unit. In so doing, he joined the ranks of many other Americans, such as Raoul Lufbery, Eddie Rickenbacker, and Frank Luke who "cut their teeth" serving with the French before joining the U.S. Air Service.[5]

While serving with the French, he earned his first aerial victory on August 8, 1918. Ten days later he transferred to the United States Air Service as a member of the 213th Aero Squadron. During his time with the 213th, his leadership skills were recognized and he was made a flight leader. Indeed, in a tribute to him, it was noted that, even during his cadet days in Tours, he was a leader to his fellow cadets.[6]

He was not only a leader but a skillful, daring and brave pilot. He earned his second "kill" on September 29 when he downed a German aircraft near Bantheville, France. He further demonstrated his skill and near recklessness on October 10 while leading a mission of four planes. Lieutenant Treadwell noticed two American observation planes being attacked by nine German planes. Ignoring the odds, he attacked the Germans who subsequently broke off the attack. This personal recklessness and concern for his fellow fliers was a hallmark of Treadie's character.

His tenacity and daring were exhibited once again on October 29, 1918 during aerial combat when he saw a German two-seater observation plane. He pursued the aircraft, firing at it and following the German as he headed for the ground to avoid further attacks. (A tactic often employed by those being pursued was to dive to the "deck" [e.g. near the ground] to shake off the pursuer with the hope that he would not descend and risk crashing himself.) Treadwell was within 50 meters of the ground, firing at the enemy. The observer was slumped over the side of the fuselage indicating he was wounded or dead. Treadwell was over German lines and was taking ground fire, but kept up the attack until his engine began giving him trouble. Only then did he break off pursuit and return to his own lines.[7]

November, 1918—The End of the War—Disaster

His story though takes a turn as the war began to wind down. The date was November 6, 1918, less than a week before the Armistice that would end the fighting of the World War. A routine mission was called for that morning, and although he was not scheduled to fly, Treadwell volunteered to go aloft, as was typical of him. He was leading a three-plane flight that included fellow Lieutenants Mell and Matheson. They were flying over Louppy-sur-Loison near Meuse, France. The location was along the Western Front, in northern France, where France borders Belgium, Luxembourg, and Germany.

Their flight path intersected that of German fighters and a short intense dogfight ensued. The fight began at approximately 5,000 feet and descended to within 30 meters of the ground. When last seen, Treadwell was descending to that 30 meter mark into a ground mist to avoid further pursuit. He was not seen after that.[8] He was reported missing in action, and word was awaited as to his fate. None was forthcoming, and after the Armistice, squadron Captain Hambleton and Lieutenant Mell went searching for Treadwell, or his aircraft. They could unearth no clues as to his fate, nor did they find his plane, a SPAD XIII.[9] It appeared that his story would remain unfinished.

Figure 1. Alvin Hill Treadwell. Died 1918. Photograph. Source unknown. On the photograph: "A First Lieutenant of the Aero Squadron. He died in France on November 16, 1918 from wounds received in action."

More to the Story

However the story did not end there. Enter the unlikely figure of Frederick Zinn. A tall, slender bespectacled native of Michigan, he seemed more suited for a bank or a classroom than a military life. His participation in the war was anything but academic. He joined the French Foreign Legion in 1914. After being wounded, he transferred to French aviation in 1916, a year before the U.S. entered the war. He served as an aerial photographer and observer. As did Treadwell, he transferred to the U.S. Air Service, ultimately serving as personnel officer. During his service he directly witnessed the loss of friends, both in the trenches and in the air some of whom went missing in action. He vowed to leave no aviator behind. Thus began his quest which would eventually lead to the discovery of the fate of Alvin Treadwell, his return home, and the completion of his story.

It is unclear as to the date Zinn's search began, but his methodical path led him first to the Red Cross. Their Frankfort office informed him that a First Lieutenant Alvin Hill Treadwell had died and was buried in Treves, Germany. Treves is near Luxembourg, and it is in this general area that Treadwell had flown on the day he was lost. Zinn then went to find the gravesite for Treadwell, and found him in grave no. 32, Stadchter Friedhof, a German military cemetery in Treves. The simple cross was marked with his name, rank, nationality, unit and date of death. The grave was also decorated with flowers. The Germans often decorated the graves of the fallen, even those of the enemy as a sign of respect. Treadwell was not forgotten, but his story was as yet unfinished.

Zinn had found Treadwell, and his family indicated that they wanted their son brought home and interred in the family plot, in Bethel, Connecticut, which is where he rests today. The family also wished to have any personal possessions of their son that may have been saved. For these, Zinn went to the Berlin Central Effects Depot. These items had been carefully inventoried and stored. The items were few, and simple: Thirteen marks, 100 Francs, a wallet, several personal letters, a receipt and his aviation insignia. Still left unknown are the events between his last flight, five days before the Armistice, and his death—as recorded—a symmetric five days after the Armistice.

So what had happened to Alvin H. Treadwell? After the war, an article printed in a Chicago newspaper brought some of the details to light. A former major who had been in a German hospital related the story of the events leading up to Treadwell's death. He had been shot through the right lower lung, the bullet entering in the back. His plane had crashed and was suspended from the top of a tree. He hung there for an unspecified period of time before he fell to the ground. He then crawled a half mile and was found by the Germans. He was brought to the ward (where the major saw him) on Armistice Day, November 11, 1918. The German doctors and nurses did what they could for him, although the wound was severe. While he was there, he was apparently both courteous and courageous, unaware perhaps of the seriousness of his condition. He laughed and joked with his fellow patients, though it was noticed that he could not eat much. He progressively became weaker, increasingly pale, and his breathing became labored. This suggests perhaps that he had been bleeding internally, but this has not been verified. The doctors gave him injections to ease his difficulty breathing and at 8:00 p.m. on November 16, 1918 he passed away. The final and as yet unsolved mystery is what happened to him from November 6 to 11.

Conclusion

The events of those five days needed to complete the story of Lieutenant Alvin Treadwell are probably lost to the fog of time. He was a soldier, pilot, son of Dutchess County, and American patriot who fought valiantly in the Great War. He is here remembered for his contribution and sacrifice.

---

[1] Peter Bedrossian ,"An annotated list of the revised Roll of Honor of War dead published in the *Poughkeepsie Eagle*, 1926," in *Dutchess County in the Great War*, 2018.

[2] "Find a Grave," in https://www.findagrave.com/memorial/43708433/alvin-hill-treadwell , *New York WWI Army Card*, https://www.fold3.com/image/591204060

[3] Amy Athey McDonald, "Defending Allied skies: Yale's pioneering pilots form first naval aviation unit," Yale News (online, 2014). https://news.yale.edu/2014/08/17/defending-allied-skies-yale-s-pioneering-pilots-form-first-naval-aviation-unit

[4] *Yale Alumni Weekly* Vol. 28, No. 18 (1919), p. 450.

[5] *Yale Alumni Weekly* Ibid., p. 426.

[6] Ibid.

[7] Blaine Pardoe, *Lost Eagles One Man's Mission To Find Missing Airmen In Two World Wars*, (Ann Arbor: University of Michigan Press, 2010).

[8] Daily Operations Report, 213th Aero Squadron, 3rdf Pursuit Group November 6, 1918 https://www.fold3.com/image/19057626?terms=alvin%20H.%20treadwell.

[9] National Museum of the Air Force, https://www.nationalmuseum.af.mil/Visit/Museum-Exhibits/Fact-Sheets/Display/Article/197399/spad-xiii-c1/.

[10] Pardoe, p. 32.

[11] Pardoe, p. 33.

[12] "Find a Grave."

[13] Pardoe, p.34.

[14] Pardoe, p. 34 and *Yale Alumni Weekly* Vol. 28, No.19 (1919), p.698.

Dutchess County's African-American Experience During the World War, 1917 to 1919...and beyond

by Bill Jeffway & Melodye K. Moore

April 1917: Call for Unity Suggests Opportunity

When President Woodrow Wilson addressed Congress in April 1917, seeking a declaration of war on Germany, he ended with a call to the nation saying, "The supreme test of the nation has come. We must all work, act, and speak together." There was "no color line," as they would have said at the time, when it came to sacrifice. Individuals of any race would be asked to suspend personal liberty and risk their lives. All were expected to sacrifice by buying war bonds, cutting back on coal consumption, and cutting back on food and basic staples like wheat and sugar. It was the pressure of the scarcity of everything, including manpower and individuals who were productive in labor or the military that created the pressure for change. The national emergency created a kind of meritocracy that opened previously closed doors to persons of color, as well as women, who stepped into new roles with a sense of urgency, and immediately performed.

Figure 1. African-American men from Dutchess County march to sign up for military service in World War I. Poughkeepsie, New York. June, 1917. Photograph by Reuben Van Vlack. Collection of the Dutchess County Historical Society. C. Fred Close Collection.

Only two divisions, the 92nd and 93rd, had Black infantry units. Of these units, the 369th, sometimes called the Harlem Hellfighters, led by Putnam County's Captain Hamilton Fish, became one of the most decorated and celebrated of the war. There were other combat units, like the 367th, in which a number of Dutchess men served. Beyond these units, many African Americans served in vital, risky, demanding, support and supply roles, as cooks, stevedores, drivers, and construction workers. A Black officer training school was created and some varied and tentative progress made. Outspoken, local proponents included Amenia's Joel Spingarn (a New York City Jewish lawyer), a co-founder of the NAACP, and Great-Barrington-born W. E. B. Dubois (an African-American writer and thinker), through his magazine *The Crisis*. This national unity and proximity put racial, and other, inequities and injustices into stark relief. How could Black men be called on to die "to make the world safe for democracy" if democracy was not practiced at home?

Figure 2. Black soldiers at Camp Whitman, Town of Beekman, Dutchess County. Photograph. Dutchess County Historical Society. L. Shook Collection. After local Dutchess County men had volunteered to serve in the War, they were first stationed at Camp Whitman in the Town of Beekman for a short stay and training before being sent onward.

June 1917: Violence is Harbinger of Resistance

In late May, only a matter of weeks after President Wilson's call for unity, violence in East St. Louis started to grow. It culminated in riots on July 3, targeting newly-arriving African Americans from the South. European immigration had virtually stopped due to the war and the growing demand for labor was accommodated by African Americans who wanted to live in the North. Several hundred Blacks were killed, thousands made homeless. One of the most vocal critics of the rioting was former President Theodore Roosevelt.

Six weeks later, on August 23 at Camp Logan in Houston, Texas, Black soldiers of the 24th Infantry Regiment encountered strictly enforced Jim Crow laws of segregation, verbal and physical abuse, and harassment by both civilians and police. They retaliated by marching on the city and killing 16 whites. Four Black soldiers died as well. Through court martial, 63 soldiers were jailed for life, and 13 were put to death by hanging.

Against this tense backdrop, Capt. Hamilton Fish arrived with Black recruits of the 369th in Spartanburg, South Carolina, in October. Soldiers were formally ordered to make no response whatsoever to the verbal and physical harassment that commenced quickly upon their arrival. As perhaps a sign of the difficult relationship they would have through their long political lives, Hamilton Fish approached Assistant Secretary of the Navy Franklin D. Roosevelt, imploring him to help get the Black servicemen back to the North. FDR took no action. It turned out that a more expedient plan was to get the troops to France earlier than planned. They went first to New York and then to France on December 17, 1917. They were among the earliest to arrive, and last to leave, in Europe.

Figure 3. Red Hook's Louis Shook mingling with locals in South Carolina while training. Dutchess County. Photograph. Collection of the Dutchess County Historical Society. L. Shook Collection.

Northern Whites, like Red Hook's Louis Shook, had a very different experience. Serving in a different unit, going to the South Carolina training camp, was a sort of curiosity. He took a number of photos showing himself meeting locals in the cotton fields (Figure 3).

Both the Newly-arrived & the Deeply-rooted Serve

Some Black recruits had only recently, and temporarily, taken up residence within Dutchess County. Both the military census and mandatory in-person registration took place in June 1917, so a number of its southern seasonal farm workers were present at the time. One such example is 23-year old David A. Clark. He was working as a temporary farm hand in the hamlet of Lafayetteville in the town of Milan, having left his parents and two sisters in his birthplace, Virginia. He departed the Poughkeepsie train station with other Black draftees on a rainy morning, October 30, 1917, never to return. Serving in the 367th Infantry, he was killed in an accidental grenade explosion on September 9, 1918, just two months before the Armistice of November 11 and is buried in France.

Figure 4. Sebie Bostic, street photo from after the War. Detail. Photograph by Reuben Van Vlack. Collection of the Dutchess County Historical Society. C. Fred Close Collection. .

Figure 5. Sebie Bostic in World War I uniform. Photograph. Collection of Bostic Family.

Others were newer arrivals but with plans to stay. Typical of what is referred to as the "great migration," Sebie Bostic had been advised by his father to move from their Georgia home to the North for his own safety, and for a greater chance of employment. (His story comes down to us from family members.) He served overseas, having been promoted to corporal in 1918 and then to sergeant in 1919. He is shown in a "street photo" with other recruits (Figure 4) and shown in uniform, from a photograph provided by his family (Figure 5). After the war he came to own his own store, and worked at a Poughkeepsie hotel spending the remainder of his life in Poughkeepsie.

By contrast, brothers Jerome and Franklin Frazier, both born in Union Vale, belonged to a long-established local family. They served their country in WWI just as their father and uncle had served from Dutchess in the Civil War, just as their northern-Dutchess based great-great grandfather Andrew Frazier had served in the Revolutionary War. Jerome and Franklin's cousin Susan Elizabeth Frazier served in WWI as the founder and president of the Women's Auxiliary of the 369th. (She is profiled below.)

The Quill was published by Poughkeepsie's Smith Metropolitan AME Zion Church. In May 1918, it thanked two of the Church's women's groups:

> Two organizations in the interest of our soldier boys have recently sprung into existence in this city, namely: "The Soldiers Comfort Club" of which Miss Grace Deyo is president, and a unit of "The Circle for Negro War Relief" with Mrs. Maggie Wormley, president. They both have worthy aims and a splendid opportunity of doing much tangible good, and merit the hearty support of one and all. They have the best wishes of *The Quill* and their very laudable undertaking. We thank you.

In the same issue, *The Quill* celebrated the success of the 369th, using its old name, the 15th, New York National Guard (see above) and decried the escalation of lynchings, writing:

> In 30 years, 3,000 Negro citizens of America whose patriotism has never been doubted; men, women and children have been butchered in almost every conceivable form by the lynching bee's and but little if any serious attention accorded it by the authorities. The sport yet goes merrily on undisturbed—four or five reported lynched the past week. ... Our boys are now abroad giving their lives for America and democracy. Can it be out of place to ask of America protection for their loved ones at home?

Gaius Bolin was the son of a Dover Plains farmer. He was the first Black graduate of Williams College and had a long and distinguished legal career, including serving as President of the Dutchess County Bar Association. The year 1919 should have been a jubilant year. Combat had ceased the prior November; the Armistice was formally signed in June 1919. Instead, it was so filled with riots that it came to be known as the "Red Summer." At its height, on August 14, Bolin wrote an open letter in the Poughkeepsie newspaper which read, in part, as follows:

> If the people of this country can afford to send the flower of its manhood, the finest men in all the world, to foreign countries to fight and suffer and die [...] they can afford to see to it that American citizenship means American citizenship, and that it means it without any kind of reservation or winking of the eye with reference to anyone who is entitled to that citizenship.

Experiences After the War

Clarence T. Anderson (Figure 6) was born in Poughkeepsie in 1893 and remained there his entire life. He married Frieda Potter April 28, 1918, just a few months before heading out to serve as a corporal at Fort Dix. After the war he settled into a 32-year career as a mail carrier, after which, he became a court officer, and was serving as such at the time of his death. Anderson was active at the Smith AME Zion Church as member, trustee, choir member, historian, Sunday school teacher, and Assistant Sunday School Superintendent.

Even with his war service, obvious strength of presence and character and skill in the community, he did not escape discrimination. In 1941, he had ordered tickets to a play in Clinton for a group of friends. Upon arrival, although

Figure 6. Clarence T. Anderson. Detail. Photograph by Reuben Van Vlack. Collection of the Dutchess County Historical Society. C. Fred Close Collection.

they could see the tickets pinned to a board behind the ticket agent, they were denied entry. A lawsuit followed which they lost. There are conflicting reports as to whether the loss was due to a procedural technicality or whether it was due to the endorsement of the validity of the counterclaim that they were denied entry "for their own safety."

George Gould (Figure 7) was born in Poughkeepsie in 1896. In the war, he served as a musician in the Regiment Band. He played piccolo, beating out five others in an audition for the one spot in the 52-person band. Music was vital in the upkeep of the morale of the troops, and relations with local civilians. He did not return from France until July 23, 1919— more than eight months after the end of fighting. When he came back, it took him five months to get a job as a bellhop at the Windsor Hotel in Poughkeepsie. In a 1979 newspaper interview with the *Poughkeepsie Journal* he said, "We weren't treated very fair when we came back. They were so prejudiced."

Figure 7. George Gould. Detail. Photograph by Reuben Van Vlack. Collection of the Dutchess County Historical Society. C. Fred Close Collection.

Susan Elizabeth Frazier's father was born in the northern Dutchess Town of Milan, part of the large family of servicemen described earlier. She herself was born in and lived in New York City. She earned a national reputation when, in 1896, she became the first person of color allowed to teach white students in New York City. Although her legal action that she had instituted had failed, her moral argument and public appeal prevailed. The story was carried in newspapers across the country. She was given a job she had for some time been denied. She became a teacher in the public schools and remained in that position until her death in 1924.

She founded and became President of the Women's Auxiliary to the 369th. In 1919, in a highly fortuitous and coincidental reflection of her

Figure 8. Well-wishers at the Poughkeepsie train station platform. July 8, 1918. Photograph by Reuben Van Vlack. Collection of the Dutchess County Historical Society. C. Fred Close Collection.

commitment to teaching and to veterans, she won a New York City newspaper contest as "favorite teacher," the prize being a trip to the battlefields of Europe. While much could be written about Miss Frazier, for our purposes here, it is worth noting the pressure she received not to go, and the constant pressure to segregate her from the main group. She died in 1924 and is buried in Rhinebeck at the family plot. In 2018, local residents raised money to erect a memorial headstone at what was her unmarked grave. Comments from newspapers at the time of her trip in 1919 reflect her strong character:

> …an effort was made to buy her off when it was discovered that she was one of the successful contestants. But she would not be bought. To all of the propositions, arguments and offers to prevent her sailing, Miss Frazier returned one answer—that she was standing on her rights as an American woman and would make the trip. On board the boat an effort to seat her at a separate table and a similar effort at the hotel in Paris were frustrated by Miss Frazier's ignoring of the plan. The officer in charge of the party, in fact, was put to the necessity of apologizing to Miss Frazier…

On her memorial headstone are the words, "Her voice endures."

[1] For an account of Dutchess County at home during World War I, see Bill Jeffway and Melodye Moore, "Over Here: The Yet-To-Be Told Stories of the Men, Women, and Children of Dutchess County During the World War, 1917 to 1919 in *Patriotism and Honor: Veterans of Dutchess County, New York, Part I; The Dutchess County Historical Society Yearbook* (vol. 97, 2018), pp. 21-37.

[2] For one account of Hamilton Fish and his participation in World War I with the Harlem Hellfighters, see Sarah Gates, "The Unknown Soldier—and the Unknown Hamilton Fish," Ibid., pp. 39-54.

[3] For an account of the formation of the NAACP, see Julia Hotton, "The Amenia Conference: The Dutchess County Connection to the Development and Growth of the NAACP," in P*rohibition and the Progressive Movement in Dutchess County, New York; The Dutchess County Historical Society Yearbook* (vol. 96, 2017), pp. 73-77.

Decoding the Past: George Wuest's First World War Adventures

by William P. Tatum III

During the summer of 2016, a mysterious package arrived at the Dutchess County Historical Society in Poughkeepsie. It contained a mix of photographs and paper ephemera, stretching from the late nineteenth century through the mid-twentieth century. There was no covering letter or identifying information with the box of items. A mystery indeed. Collections Committee Chair Melodye Moore's careful sleuthing revealed the material to be the final bequest of Beulah Wuest, who had passed away several years prior without an heir. After dutifully following the conditions of her last will and testament, the law office charged with settling her estate had gathered up the remaining family photographs and paperwork, and had now sent them to the Clinton House to be placed on deposit for future generations of researchers.

Unraveling a Mystery: Beulah Wuest and her husband, George Wuest

Melodye Moore's continuing research soon uncovered the outlines of Beulah Wuest's personal history. Born Beulah Gale Boice, the later Mrs. Wuest grew up as part of an established farming family in Red Hook with ties throughout northern Dutchess County. Photographs of nineteenth-century farms and paperwork from the Dutchess County Fair that appear in the collection testify to the family's deep roots in the local agricultural community. Interspersed with these childhood memories and later material relating to life in Poughkeepsie from the 1920s through the 1950s is a set of small black-and-white photos of the World War I era. These items, along with other scattered ephemera, chronicle the life of Beulah's husband, George Wuest, who pre-deceased her in 1974. Analyzing George's pictorial chronicle of his time in the army provides a window into an otherwise forgotten part of Dutchess County's experience of the "Great War."

Our information on George Wuest's pre-war life comes from his official service card, preserved in the New York State Archives, and his obituary published in the *Poughkeepsie Journal*. Wuest was born in New York City to Henry and Barbara (nee Werner) Wuest on March 17,1888. He attended the Pratt Institute and, by 1917, had established a summer home in Rhinebeck. Army officers inducted him into the service there on March 8, 1918. He served with the 62nd Provisional Truck Company until July 7, 1918, then transferred to the newly-formed air service (at this time still part of the army). He initially joined the 609th Aero Supply Squadron, then transferred to the 880th Aero Squadron on July 11, 1918, in which he would continue until his discharge in 1919 (Figure 1).

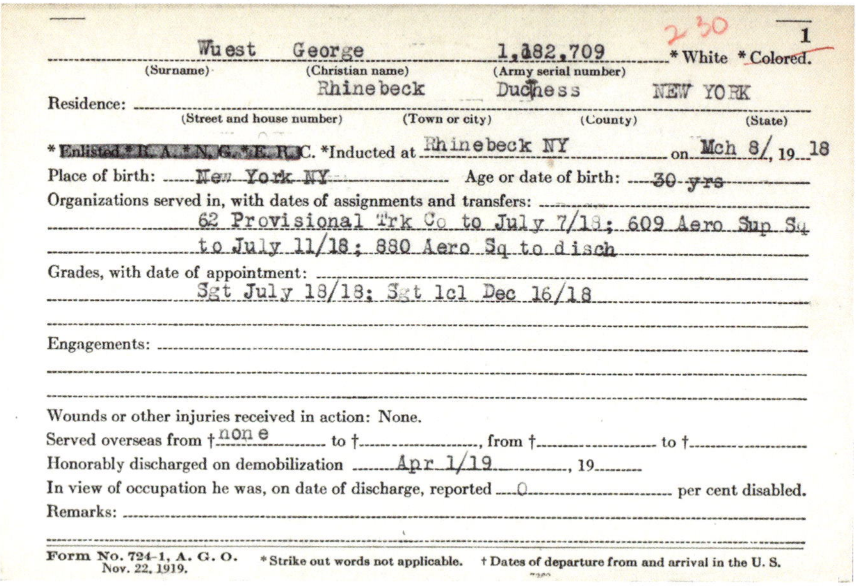
2 30 1

Wuest George 1,482,709 * White ~~*Colored.~~
(Surname) (Christian name) (Army serial number)

Residence: Rhinebeck Duchess NEW YORK
(Street and house number) (Town or city) (County) (State)

~~*Enlisted *R. A. *N. G. *E. R. C.~~ *Inducted at Rhinebeck NY on Mch 8/, 19 18

Place of birth: New York NY Age or date of birth: 30 yrs

Organizations served in, with dates of assignments and transfers:
62 Provisional Trk Co to July 7/18; 609 Aero Sup Sq
to July 11/18; 880 Aero Sq to disch

Grades, with date of appointment:
Sgt July 18/18; Sgt 1cl Dec 16/18

Engagements:

Wounds or other injuries received in action: None.

Served overseas from †none to †, from † to †

Honorably discharged on demobilization Apr 1/19, 19

In view of occupation he was, on date of discharge, reported 0 per cent disabled.

Remarks:

Form No. 724-1, A. G. O. Nov. 22, 1919. *Strike out words not applicable. †Dates of departure from and arrival in the U. S.

Figure 1. George Wuest's Service Card for World War I. Honorably discharged on demobilization, April 1, 1919. Collection of the Dutchess County Historical Society.

Decoding George Wuest's Photographs

The history of the latter two units provides the key for decoding George Wuest's engaging photographs. The U.S. Army Air Service formed the 609th Squadron at Kelly Field, Texas, in January 1918. The unit was part of the army's supply services and transferred its headquarters to Mitchel Field (now Mitchel Air Force Base) at Uniondale, New York, on Long Island. The air service organized the 880th Squadron in June 1918 at Montgomery, Alabama, where it would remain until disbandment in March 1919. The 880th operated as a repair unit at Aviation Depot Number 3 (now Maxwell Air Force Base). A letter included in the Wuest Collection helps to explain George's enrollment in the provisional truck company and the two aero squadrons, as well as his meteoric rise from private to sergeant. On March 19, 1918, William H. Judson, Cashier of the First National Bank in Rhinebeck, dictated a recommendation letter for Wuest. Judson stated that he had known Wuest for four years, during which time Wuest had served as foreman "in the shop of Turton & Snyder." Judson recommended Wuest as a thorough, capable, conscientious careful and honest workeman [sic]" and expressed his confidence that Wuest would ably fill any position.

A report of the New York State Public Service Commission from April 1914 identifies Turton & Snyder as a Rhinebeck-based company that operated an "auto bus line" between the train station at Rhinecliff and the village. As foreman of the shop, Wuest would have gained practical experience to supplement his education at the Pratt Institute, making him an excellent candidate for the highly technical work of repairing aircraft. Wuest's civilian experience likely drove his promotion directly to sergeant on July 18, 1918: having been in service for less than two months, the 880th Aero Squadron was likely in need of skilled and experienced leaders.

George Wuest's Service

Wuest's photographs of his World War I service all seem to date from his time in the 880th Aero Squadron. The images offer glimpses into camp life, an excursion to the state capital at Montgomery, and views of the airplanes upon which Wuest and his fellow soldiers worked. The exact

Figure 2. George Wuest in uniform. n.d. Photograph. Collection of the Dutchess County Historical Society. The sergeant's stripes on his sleeve indicate that the photo was taken after his promotion in July 1918. This portrait has provided our key for identifying Wuest in subsequent images.

chronology of these photographs, however, is difficult to establish. Only half of the collection features any kind of identifying data recorded on the photographs—short notes on the obverse side providing pithy commentary. From the phrasing, it seems likely that Wuest sent these images home and that the commentary was intended for the recipients, potentially his parents in New York City. The only dated image (Figure 3) captures Wuest standing on a river bank holding a piece of cotton, alongside an unnamed soldier with sergeant's stripes. The note on the reverse of this photograph records that "G.A.A. of Brooklyn" took it on Sunday, November 10, 1918, the day before the Central and Allied Powers declared a general armistice. The note further observes that it was a "hot day about 90°."

Figure 3. George Wuest and an unknown sergeant on November 10, 1918. Photograph. Collection of the Dutchess County Historical Society. On the back of the photograph is a note: "G.A.A. of Brooklyn" took it on Sunday, November 10, 1918, a "hot day about 90 degrees."

A set of four photographs captures scenes of camp life, although no identification is provided on when they were taken or where the camp was located. The clear presence of snow indicates a late fall/winter/early spring date. Considering Wuest's dates of service, these photographs most likely date from the autumn of 1918 into the winter of 1918-1919. The first image (Figure 4) captures a group of men erecting a winter shelter in a military camp.

Figure 4. George Wuest and companions erecting a winter tent at military camp. Date probably fall 1918. Location of camp not clear. Photograph. Collection of the Dutchess County Historical Society.

Figure 5. Camp life, rising in the morning. Winter, 1918-1919. Photograph. Collection of the Dutchess County Historical Society. A soldier is calling soldiers to rise at 6 a.m. and issuing orders.

Wuest's note on the reverse boldly states that this was the best tent in their section of the camp: "floor and siding are issued, the rest of lumber we stole." The army still provided cotton canvas tents as year-round shelter in the field at this time, much as it had during the previous conflicts dating back to the mid-nineteenth century. The practice of reinforcing these tents for winter occupancy by building a board or log foundation and partial sides had, by World War One, become semi-official practice, as Wuest notes. However, the amount of timber that the army provided to reinforce the tent cloth was insufficient for insuring the warmest quarters, hence Wuest's resorting to the time-honored military tradition of theft. This winterizing treatment indicates that the photo was likely taken in the autumn of 1918, shortly before the onset of cold weather. Therefore this camp was likely located near Maxwell Field, though available photos of that facility do not indicate an adjacent camp of this style.

The next photo in this camp-themed set (Figure 5) records the onset of winter. A soldier wearing a winter greatcoat over his uniform and sporting the signature broad-brimmed campaign hat stands on a platform, speaking into a megaphone. Wuest's note on the reverse identifies this soldier as the "guy that takes all the job out of army life, especially at 6 A.M. each morning." Presumably this soldier is rousing the base and issuing out the morning orders and announcements.

Figure 6. Three comrade soldiers pose in front of the Alabama Capital building: Livingston, Colton, and Wuest. Date probably late winter 1919. Photograph. Ohio Photo Studio company of Montgomery, Alabama. Collection of the Dutchess County Historical Society.

Figure 7. Civilians gather around a Curtiss JN-4 "Jenny," a training airplane for military pilots. Date probably 1919. Photograph. Collection of the Dutchess County Historical Society.

The final two images are both landscape views of the camp. The first shows two lines of snow-covered tents facing each other across a broad avenue. In his note on the reverse, Wuest observes that this is a view of his "company street" in "The Sunny South" a few days earlier. He goes on to describe the snow as "some bunch of cotton," no doubt reflecting the irony that many soldiers felt on facing stereotypically northern weather in such a southerly climate. The final photo is, as Wuest notes on the observe, a view from the back of the camp, including the "showers, latrines, and horse picket line," the latter probably for officers' horses. The winter of 1918-1919 was an unusually cold one, as a study published in the *Bulletin of the American Meteorological Society* revealed in 2010. It is likely that this extreme weather contributed to the influenza epidemic that swept across the planet that winter, though it seems to have left George Wuest untouched.

The remaining photographs from World War I in the Wuest Collection can be split between the themes of field excursions and Wuest's work on aircraft. Unfortunately, most of these images lack explanatory notes. The first set begins with a picture postcard from the Ohio Photo Studio Company of Montgomery, Alabama. The image shows three soldiers standing in front of the Alabama capital building (Figure 6). Wuest has written their surnames below each man: "Livingston- Colton- Wuest." Each man carries a winter greatcoat over his arm and the trees in the background are mostly bereft of leaves, suggesting a fall or early spring date. The following two images of the field excursion set depict a airplane without wings sitting on a municipal street, surrounded by civilians. The trees are similarly bereft of leaves, suggesting that perhaps the three images were taken around the same time. Perhaps Wuest's unit brought an airplane under repair to Montgomery as a public relations program and stopped to have their photograph taken at the state capital? The aircraft pictured (Figure 7) is a Curtiss JN-4 "Jenny," originaly produced as a training airplane for military pilots, which continued in civilian service after the war.

Figure 8. View of airplane (close-up of engine). n.d., probably 1919. Photograph. Collection of the Dutchess County Historical Society. Note on reverse: "Scout plane, with Gnome motor." Probably a Thomas=Morse S-4 "Scout," a training airplane.

Six photographs comprise the set covering Wuest's work on aircraft. Of these, only one has an explanatory note. That image captures a close-up view of an airplane, focusing on its engine (Figure 8). The note on the reverse reads "Scout plane, with Gnome motor." The airplane is most likely a Thomas-Morse S-4 "Scout," another training aircraft of the period. A second photograph shows an engine on a test stand, while the remaining four provide different views of a JN-4. Two of these include mechanics posing with the plane: one view has Wuest standing in front of it alone, while the other includes three other mechanics, none of whom are identified (Figure 9).

Figure 9. George Wuest with three comrades in front of a NJ-4 plane. n.d., probably 1919. Photograph. Collection of the Dutchess County Historical Society.

Return to Civilian Life

George Wuest's military service concluded on April 1, 1919, when the army honorably discharged him as part of a general post-war demobilization. His experience of World War One, as seen through these photos, is not the stuff of horrific trench warfare. Nevertheless, his collection provides an important reminder of the men who served in the United States, providing vital supplies and support for the war effort in Europe. George Wuest's experience reminds us that war is not a phenomenon limited to the theatre of actual fighting, but rather touches all parts of our society.

While George Wuest's war concluded in April 1919, his life did not end there. Returning to New York, he seems to have split his time between Dutchess County and New York City until the late 1920s. The New York State census of 1925 records Wuest as a full time resident of his parents' home at 3562 Park Avenue. Shortly after the census, Wuest moved to 21 Cedar Avenue in the city of Poughkeepsie full-time. By 1935, he and Beulah had married, and George became involved in Poughkeepsie politics, unsuccessfully running for 8th Ward Alderman that year. In December, Poughkeepsie Mayor George V.L. Spratt appointed Wuest to the Board of Public Welfare. Wuest ran again for 8th Ward alderman in 1937, but suffered defeat. On Thursday, December 1, 1938, the Poughkeepsie Taxpayers Association elected Wuest to be vice-president, leading to his resignation from the welfare board. In 1942, Wuest served as warden for the 8th Ward and organized a scrap drive to support the Second World War effort.

Wuest's long and eventful life came to a close on January 29, 1974, when he passed away at the Veterans Administration Hospital at Castle Point. His obituary recorded that he had worked as a production engineer at the DeLaval Separator Company in Poughkeepsie, and been an active member of the First Baptist Church and the Lafayette Post of the American Legion. He was survived by his wife, Beulah, and his niece, Professor Carolyn Eisele of New York City. An undated photograph in the Wuest Papers (Figure 10) provides us with a potential final view of George and Beulah together, likely taken at their home in Poughkeepsie—a fitting tribute to a Dutchess County family whose story is now forever preserved with the county historical society.

Figure 10. George and Beulah Wuest, late in life, at their Poughkeepsie home on Cedar Avenue. n.d. Photograph. Collection of the Dutchess County Historical Society.

[1] "George Wuest," *The Poughkeepsie Journal*, Thursday, January 31, 1974, pg 25; "Moore to Remain on Police Board; Hey to Succeed Owen on B.P.W.; Wuest Chosen to Replace Joseph," *Poughkeepsie Eagle-News*, Tuesday, Dec 31, 1935, pg 1, 4; George Wuest Service Card, New York State Archives Ancestry.com. New York, *Abstracts of World War I Military Service*, 1917-1919 [database on-line]. Provo, UT, USA: Ancestry.com Operations, Inc., 2013.

[2] *Order of Battle of the United States Land Forces in the First World War,* Volume 3, Part 3, Center of Military History, United States Army, 1949 (1988 Reprint).

[3] William H. Judson to Whom it may concern, March 18, 1918, Rhinebeck, NY, Wuest Collection, Dutchess County Historical Society.

[4] Case Number 4226, State of New York, *8th Annual Report of the Public Service Commission Second District for the Year Ended December 31, 1914*, Volume I, Albany: 1915.

[5] Frederick C. Gaede, *The Federal Civil War Shelter Tent*, Alexandria, VA: O'Donnell Publications, 2001.

[6] 100 Years of Service: Alabama base educates the Air Force, boosts state economy," http://alabamaliving.coop/article/100-years-of-service/, accessed April 18, 2019.

[7] Benjamin S. Giese et al, "The 1918/19 El Niño, *Bulletin of the American Meteorological Society*, February 2010, https://doi.org/10.1175/2009BAMS2903.1.

[8] All aircraft identification provided by David Niescior of the Old Barracks Museum, Trenton, NJ.

[9] New York State Archives, Ancestry.com. *New York, State Census*, 1925 [database on-line]. Provo, UT, USA: Ancestry.com Operations, Inc., 2012.A.D. 02 E.D. 44; "Moore to Remain on Police Board; Hey to Succeed Owen on B.P.W.; Wuest Chosen to Replace Joseph," *Poughkeepsie Eagle-News*, Tuesday, Dec 31, 1935, pg 1 and 4; "Spratt and Graham Named to Head Democratic Slate as Party Attains Harmony," Wednesday, Aug 4, 1937, pgs 1-2; "Member of the Next Common Council Chosen at Yesterday's Election in Poughkeepsie," *Poughkeepsie Eagle-News*, Nov 3, 1937, pg 8; "Good Move- Neutral in Nothing," *Poughkeepsie Eagle-News*, Dec 2, 1938, pg 6; "Daily Scrap Collections to End in Eighth Ward," *Poughkeepsie Eagle-News*, Saturday, October 17, 1942.

[10] *The Poughkeepsie Journal*, Thursday, January 31, 1974, pg 25.

Immigrant Farmer in the OSS

by Julian Strauss

My father, William J. Strauss, (1912- 1979) served his country in World War II as a soldier in the U.S. Army and as a member of a special forces group in the Office of Strategic Services (OSS).

Figure 1. William Julian Strauss in his World War II uniform, at his farm in Amenia, New York after the war, 1945. Photograph. Collection of Julian Strauss.

Willy Julian Strauss was born and educated in the city of Frankfurt, Germany. He considered himself to be an "assimilated," secular Jew from a prosperous family. His position in the family business was secure. His father and several uncles ran a factory processing animal parts, for example the hoofs and other cast-off parts, into usable products such as felt and glue. They were limited to this profession by German law, but had made the work profitable with a substantial number of employees and many local and overseas customers. Willy himself had almost no involvement in the business. He had little direct contact with the business except for a trip at age 19 to Eastman Kodak in Rochester, New York to sell Celluloid for photographic film. I am not sure exactly what my father, as a 20-year-old, was thinking when he made his decision to leave Germany, except to know that he didn't like the business world and the Nazi ideology that was beginning the grow there. He might have been moved by a "Back to the land" emotion, without the full realization of what that involved. If there is one thing that could be said about Willy, later Bill Strauss, it is that, throughout his life, he had a driving desire to return to the land and to have contact with animals. He was denied this goal in Germany, so he began to look for change. In 1933, therefore, when he turned 21, he decided to start a new life elsewhere.

It was at that time in 1933, that Adolph Hitler passed anti-Jewish legislation, which deprived the Jews of their freedoms. Hitler decreed that Jews were no longer permitted to pursue certain activities, such as Willy's hobby of flying gliders and airplanes. William could see "the handwriting on the wall," so to speak, and consequently determined to leave Europe. He went first to France to study agriculture, a profession also forbidden by decree to the Jews in Germany. While in college at Grinon, he met my mother, Elizabeth, who was a nursing student in Paris.

Figure 2. Bill Strauss Farming at Home farm in Amenia, New York, 1940. Photo. Collection of Julian Strauss.

Immigration to the United States

In late 1935, during the peak of the Great Depression, William and Elizabeth Strauss immigrated to the United States. They came to New York, to Dutchess County, and bought a dairy farm on the border of the towns of Amenia and North East. I was born a few months later in 1936.

My childhood memories are in the context of the Depression, as well as the outbreak and progress of WWII. As a small boy, I remember returning from a trip to France with my mother on the *USS Normandie*, just after the German invasion of Poland, in the autumn of 1939. In 1940, when Paris fell, I imagine that there were serious conversations in French around our kitchen table. I vividly remember the announcement of the Japanese attack on Pearl Harbor in December 1941 and Father's declaration to friends, "This means war."

Figure 3. Bill Strauss in Uniform, 1943. Photo. Collection of Julian Strauss.

William, also known as Bill, immediately wanted to enlist in the army. He was refused in 1941, because he was considered to be an enemy alien. In actual fact, he was a stateless person. He had lost his German citizenship by the Nazi government's decree that Jews were no longer Germans. In early 1943, however, the draft board called him. Although William was 31 years old, a farmer, married, and with children, he wanted to serve in the military.

Service in the U.S. Army and the OSS

Because he had had flying experience, Bill's first assignment in the U.S. Army was as an Airplane Maintenance Technician at Camp Butner, North Carolina. I remember how proud I was when Mother and I visited him at the camp.

My mother understood my father's sense of duty to fight for liberty in Europe and to identify as an American, even though he was not yet a full-fledged citizen. However, his absence from the farm and the family put a great burden on her shoulders. During the next two years, her life was not easy as she had to manage the farm with a hired man, work part time as a nurse and care for an infant, a handicapped child and me.

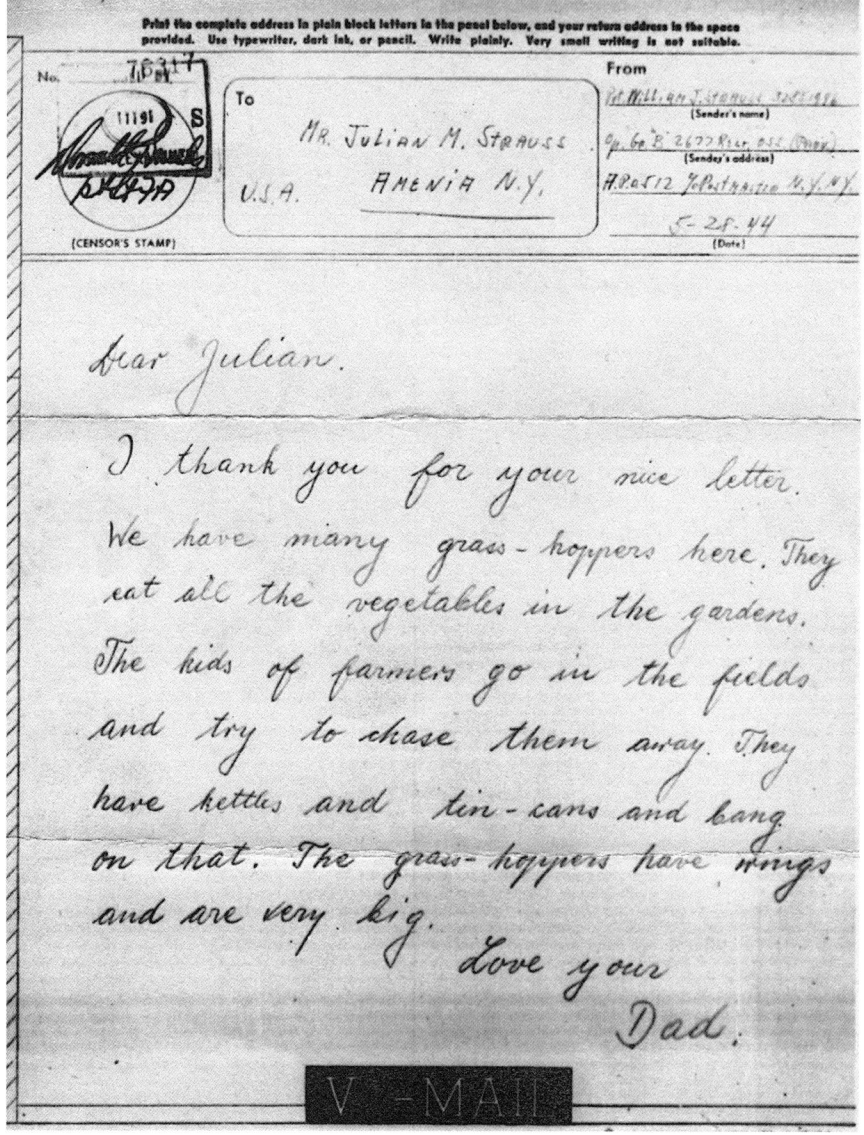

> Dear Julian,
>
> I thank you for your nice letter. We have many grass-hoppers here. They eat all the vegetables in the gardens. The kids of farmers go in the fields and try to chase them away. They have kettles and tin-cans and bang on that. The grass-hoppers have wings and are very big.
>
> Love your
> Dad.

Figure 4. V Letter from Bill Strauss to son Julian, 1944. Collection of Julian Strauss.

While working at Camp Butner, William Strauss received an unexpected visit from an army officer who began to speak to him in German and then in French. He was asked if he would be interested in volunteering for hazardous duty behind enemy lines. He was made to understand that this assignment would involve dangerous situations. William expressed a desire to be part of such an assignment and to serve in a new branch of the military, the Office of Strategic Services (OSS). Within 24 hours, William Strauss was declared a citizen of the United States.

For the next year and a half, my father essentially "disappeared" from his family. The only time I heard from him was through a censored "V Letter" in the spring of 1944.

Figure 5. OG PEG, 1944 (T/5 Bill Strauss, front row, 2nd from right) (OG PEG= Operational Group, code named "PEG" in action in Carcassonne, France, 1944). Photo. Collection of Julian Strauss.

Years later, my father told me, with a chuckle, that from Camp Butner he was sent to the Congressional Country Club in Washington, DC. That was where the OSS conducted training for the new recruits. William was assigned to be a part of an Operational Group (OG). There were dozens of such small groups. His group, code named "PEG" was to eventually go to France.

Basic OG training was based on physical conditioning, hand to hand combat, special weapons use, including the 45-caliber pistol and the stiletto. All OG soldiers had training in map reading, compass use and night operations for scouting and reconnaissance, for hit and run commando tactics. They all had training in demolitions and, of course, for survival, living off the land.[1] My father was trained to operate a clandestine radio.

OG PEG crossed the Atlantic by ship to its base in North Africa. There the unit continued its training in parachute jumping techniques from different types of planes, learning how to jump from the belly of the plane where the gunners' turret would normally be located.

The mission of OG PEG, which included my father, T/5 William Strauss, was to harass the enemy forces by cutting off Route National 117 and by destroying communication and supply lines in the Carcassonne Gap. The Group was also to bring supplies and weapons to the Maquis, the French Resistance group in that area which would assist in the overall mission.

Figure 6. Bill Strauss in uniform, in Grenoble, France, 1944. Photo. Collection of Julian Strauss.

U. S. Army OG PEG (*Operational Group Code Named "PEG"*) in Action in Carcassonne, France, 1944

The following chronological information is used by permission from the Historical Society of the Maquis of Aude located in Carcassonne, France. I have added bits of detail that I learned directly from my father over the years following the war.

11 August 1944

The OG PEG left Blida Airport in North Africa at 0300 hours for the Aude River area of France near Axat. Flying was good, so that some of the soldiers were able to sleep on the flight. The Drop Zone, was 12 miles from the one intended and was suitable for equipment but not personnel. Mountains prevented flying low. Because of the higher than usual altitude of approach the drop zone was extended over a larger area. The men landed among trees and rock formations. Three men were injured but not so serious that they could not keep up with the Section. T/5 Strauss had two fractured ribs and a wrenched shoulder, but he carried on with the mission, carrying arms, munitions, and other supplies to the Maquis' hiding places.

William Strauss was Number 2 in the string of jumpers to drop through the hole of the Lancaster bomber. The order to jump came only after small fires lit by the Maquis and their vehicle headlights were spotted. My father recalled taking out his eyeglasses from his vest pocket on descent to scout the ground as best he could, and then replacing them in his pocket.

12-13 August

The day was spent opening containers and cleaning weapons, while officers and others did reconnaissance in the area. At night, a railroad bridge between Carcassonne and Rive Saltes, which had been in continual use by German supply trains, was destroyed.

14 August

The day was spent teaching the Maquis how to use the weapons.

That night, the Section destroyed three stone arch bridges, completely cutting off access to Route Nationale 117 and one bypass.

16 August

The day was spent strengthening defence around village of Salvezines. The roads were mined and machine guns were placed in strategic positions.

Maquis force increased from 40 to 250 men. Lack of arms prevented others from joining.

17 August

While placing demolition to block a road near Alet, a detail of Maquis and four OGs were met by Germans. As Lt. Swank and Sgt. Galley delayed the Germans' approach with gunfire, so that the others could escape, the Lieutenant was shot down. The others continued fire and turned back the enemy, killing 19 and wounding four. Only two Maquis were killed, and two Maquis and two OGs were wounded.

The OGs rejoined the rest of the Section at night except for T/5 Veilleux. Veilleux had become separated from the Group. He was fired on by three of the enemy and fell into a ditch as though dead. When the three Germans approached, he opened fire and killed all three without injury to himself.

18 August

We spent the day burying Lt. Swank and taking care of the wounded. The townspeople prepared a lavish funeral service for Lt. Swank and the two Maquis members who had been killed, with a truckload of flowers and military honors.

19 August

We were to have attacked a warehouse today, but the enemy heard rumors that 500 American parachutists had landed. When we arrived at the warehouse, the guards had already surrendered. The food from the warehouse,- sufficient enough to feed 100,000 troops, was distributed to the nearby towns. We moved on to Limoux where we could wash clothes and rest. We stayed there three days. A Jedburg team, a different kind of OSS group, asked for our help in wrecking a German troop train leaving Carcassonne. When we arrived at the place we were too late for the train, but we tore up the tracks, so that the enemy would not be able to use them for retreat.

Figure 7. OG PEG in Victory March, August 1944. Photo. Collection of Julian Strauss.

23 August

Our Maquis guard at Limoux was attacked by 32 Germans trying to escape to Spain. The Section joined the guard and a detail of OGs under S/Sgt. Sampson, who had taken Lt. Swank's place. By a flanking action, we forced the enemy to surrender after a half-hour battle. The Section subsequently headed north laying ambushes and encouraging Maquis resistance forces to fight enemy bands trying to reach Spain.

Section next headed east to Allied Forces who had pushed north of the Section. We met the French Army at Montpellier and American Forces at Avignon, and then continued on to Grenoble to report to headquarters. (end of chronological report)[2]

After the War: Looking Back

All activities of the OSS were considered top secret and to this date there are many questions that remain unanswered. My father was reluctant to talk much about his training and his war experiences, even decades after the war.

William Strauss' separation papers cryptically summarized his military experience in this manner: *"Intelligence N.C.O.—Worked with organization requiring paratroop training in execution of confidential assignment."*

One of the men in OG PEG who considered himself a close buddy of Bill Strauss was T/5 Jean Kohn. Jean Kohn, son of French Jewish refugees, was an 18-year-old college student in Syracuse when he was drafted. After the War, he and his parents visited Bill at Home Farm in Amenia.

In 2004, Jean was living in Paris, France. At that time, he was writing his memoires and contacted my sister, Eva, who also lives in Paris. Through Jean, we learned of his experiences in the OSS. He told us of how he went back to Carcassonne in recent years and found the pistol he had hidden in the ground under a tree in August of 1944, when escaping from the Germans. His story is now in a book which is available online.[3]

The mission of OG PEG in the Aude River and the Carcassonne region was a classic example of how the newly developed effectiveness of the radio, the airplane and the parachute were used by an OG to equip and organize a partisan guerilla force and to perform a coordinated plan of attack. In all this, William Strauss, with his language ability and newly acquired skills as radio operator and demolitions technician, accomplished what he desired to do, that is, to strike a blow against Hitler for the sake of his new country.

Figure 8. Jean Kohn and Bill Strauss with young Julian in Amenia, 1945. Photo. Collection of Julian Strauss.

Conclusion

For a proud new American citizen, one who had been raised as an "assimilated" German Jew and had grown up with German friends who were later forced to fight for Hitler, this victorious war experience came at a great emotional price. Having to interrogate captured German soldiers and carry out the necessary commands haunted my father for the rest of his life. Bill Strauss, husband, father and farmer, was troubled by the horrors of war and by what he had witnessed. His marriage and his children suffered, too, as a consequence of his war experience. Unfortunately, they did not "live happily ever after." Although it was hard to readjust to life after the War, Bill was proud to have served with the OSS and proud of his part in the defeat of Hitler's Third Reich. In addition, in spite of some quite significant disappointments in his life, my father Bill Strauss was always possessed of his enormous love of the land and of farming. These he had been denied in Germany. Pursuing them had been essentially impossible in pre-war France, but a dream come true in America in little, bucolic Amenia, New York. Bill lived out his life on the farm in Amenia. I was with him. I am there still.

Figure 9. Purple Heart awarded to William J. Strauss. Photo. Collection of Julian Strauss.

---

[1] Nathan C. Hill, "Sowing Dragon's Teeth," pp32-33, in *Military Review*, July-August 2013. Available online at www.armyupress.army.mil

[2] Maquis FTP Jean Robert & Faita, "Anti-Nazi Resistance in the Aude River Upper Valley," available at maquisftp-jeanrobert-faita.org

[3] Jean Kohn, *A Civilian in Uniform, 1943-1945*, self-published book, 56 pages. Available online at oss-og.org.

"Orchestrated Hell"

Edward R. Murrow's December 1943 radio broadcast, reporting on his RAF bomber flight over Nazi Germany

with commentary by John Barry

Figure 1. Edward R. Murrow. Correspondent for CBS World News. Shown in American military uniform as he dressed when accompanying crews on flights over the English Channel and the European continent on bombing missions into Germany in 1943 and 1944. Photograph. Washington State University, wsu.edu.

Introduction by John Barry

During the Second World War, Edward R. Murrow, the famous Pawling resident, was a frequent veteran of combat against Nazi Germany.

Murrow flew on 25 combat sorties with the British Royal Air Force over Nazi-controlled Europe, and frequently stood unprotected on the roof of the Broadcast House in London in 1940, microphone in hand, as the German Luftwaffe dropped bombs all over the city, to broadcast live radio reports about "The Blitz" to his American audience.

Given the high casualty rate on those RAF missions at the height of the war, the odds were against surviving the 25 missions that Murrow flew on. The pilot of the mission Murrow describes below, Jock Abercrombie, was shot down and killed the following month. Only a few fellow reporters risked their lives this way.

Murrow was a knowledgeable American reporter and patriot. He thoroughly understood and firmly believed in the liberal values that the war was being fought to defend and preserve. From observing the Nazis at close range in the 1930s and early 1940s, he understood what was at stake in the struggle against Nazism and the German nation under its thrall. For the same reason, after the war, Murrow later confronted and helped expose the malicious illiberal and politically expedient slanders of Senator Joseph McCarthy at a time when much of the press establishment of that day aided and abetted him.

What follows is Murrow's description of the first of what became his twenty-five bombing missions, transcribed from the 3 December 1943 Columbia Broadcasting System broadcast under the title "Orchestrated Hell." A personal postscript follows this broadcast transcript.—J. Barry

CBS Announcer: CBS World News now brings you a special broadcast from London. Columbia's correspondent, Edward R. Murrow, was on one of the RAF bombing planes that smashed at Berlin last night, in one of the heaviest attacks of the war. Forty-one bombers were lost in the raid and three out of the five correspondents who flew with the raiders failed to return. For Mr. Murrow's story of the attack, we take you now to London.

Murrow: This is London. Last night, some of the young gentlemen of the RAF took me to Berlin. The pilot was called Jock Abercrombie. The crew captains walked into the briefing room, looked at the maps and charts, and sat down with their big celluloid pads on their knees. The atmosphere was that of a school and a church. The weatherman gave us the weather. The pilots were reminded that Berlin is Germany's greatest center of war production. The intelligence officer told us how many heavy and light ack-ack guns, how many searchlights we might expect to encounter. Then, Jock, the wing commander, explained the system of markings, the kind of flares that would be used by the pathfinders. He said that concentration was the secret of success in these raids; that as long as the aircraft stayed well-bunched, they would protect each other.

The captains of aircraft walked out. I noticed that the big Canadian with the slow, easy grin had printed "Berlin" at the top of his pad and then embellished it with a scroll. The red-headed English boy with the two-weeks'-old mustache was the last to leave the room.

Late in the afternoon we went to the locker room to draw parachutes, Mae Wests[1] and all the rest. As we dressed, a couple of the Australians were whistling. Walking out to the bus that was to take us to the aircraft, I heard the station loudspeakers announcing that that evening all personnel would be able to see a film, *Star-Spangled Rhythm*—free.

We went out and stood around the big, black four-motored Lancaster, "D for Dog." A small station wagon delivered a thermos bottle of coffee, chewing gum, an orange, and a bit of chocolate for each man. Up in that part of England the air hums and throbs with the sound of aircraft motors all day, but for half an hour before takeoff the skies are dead, silent, and expectant. A lone hawk hovered over the airfield, absolutely still as he faced into the wind. Jack, the tail gunner, said, "It'd be nice to fly like that." D-Dog eased around the perimeter track to the end of the runway. We sat there for a moment. The green light flashed and we were rolling—ten seconds ahead of schedule.

Figure 2. Lancansters in flight. English bombers, World War II. Photograph. Wikipedia.org.

The takeoff was smooth as silk. The wheels came up, and D-Dog started the long climb. As we came up through the clouds, I looked right and left and counted fourteen black Lancasters climbing for the place where men must burn oxygen to live. The sun was going down and its red glow made rivers of lakes of fire on tops of the clouds. Down to the southward, the clouds piled up to form castles, battlements, and whole cities, all tinged with red.

Soon we were out over the North Sea. Dave, the navigator, asked Jock if he couldn't make a little more speed. We were nearly two minutes late. By this time, we were all using oxygen. The talk on the intercom was brief and crisp. Everyone sounded relaxed. For a while, the eight of us in our little world in exile moved over the sea. There was a quarter moon on the starboard beam and Jock's quiet voice came through the intercom, "That'll be flak ahead." We were approaching the enemy coast. The flak looked like a cigarette lighter in a dark room— one that won't light, sparks but no flame— the sparks crackling just above the level of the cloud tops. We flew steady and straight, and soon the flak was directly below us. D-Dog rocked a little from right to left, but that wasn't caused by the flak. We were in the slipstream of other Lancasters ahead, and we were over the enemy coast.

And then a strange thing happened. The aircraft seemed to grow smaller. Jack in the rear turret, Wally the mid-upper gunner, Titch the wireless operator, all seemed somehow to draw closer to Jock in the cockpit. It was as though each man's shoulder was against the others. The understanding was complete. The intercom came to life, and Jock said, "Two aircraft on the port beam." Jack in the tail said, "Okay, sir. They're Lancs." The whole crew was a unit and wasn't wasting words.

The cloud below was ten-tenths. The blue-green jet of the exhausts licked back along the leading edge, and there were other aircraft all around us. The whole great aerial armada was hurtling towards Berlin. We flew so for twenty minutes, when Jock looked up at a vapor trail curling across above us, remarking in a conversational tone that, from the look of it, he thought there was a fighter up there. Occasionally the angry red of ack-ack burst through the clouds, but it was far away, and we took only an academic interest. We were flying in the third wave.

Jock asked Wally in the mid-upper turret, and Jack in the rear turret, if they were cold. They said they were all right and thanked him for asking. He even asked how I was and I said, "All right so far." The cloud was beginning to thin out. Off to the north we could see lights, and the flak began to liven up ahead of us. Buzz, the bomb-aimer, crackled through on the intercom, "There's a battle going on the starboard beam." We couldn't see the aircraft, but we could see the jets of red tracer being exchanged. Suddenly, there was a burst of yellow flame and Jock remarked, "That's a fighter going down. Note the position." The whole thing was interesting, but remote. Dave, the navigator, who was sitting back with his maps, charts, and compasses, said, "The attack ought to begin in exactly two minutes." We were still over the clouds.

But suddenly those dirty gray clouds turned white and we were over the outer searchlight defenses. The clouds below us were white, and we were black. D-Dog seemed like a black bug on a white sheet. The flak began coming up, but none of it close. We were still a long way from Berlin. I didn't realize just how far. Jock observed, "There's a kite on fire dead ahead." It was a great, golden, slow-moving meteor slanting toward the earth. By this time we were about thirty miles from our target area in Berlin. That thirty miles was the longest flight I have ever made.

Dead on time, Buzz the bomb-aimer reported, "Target indicators going down." At the same moment, the sky ahead was lit up by bright yellow flares. Off to starboard another kite went down in flames. The flares were sprouting all over the sky, reds and greens and yellows, and we were flying straight for the center of the fireworks. D-Dog seemed to be standing still, the four propellers thrashing the air, but we didn't seem to be closing in. The clouds had cleared, and off to the starboard a Lanc was caught by at least fourteen searchlight beams. We could see him twist and turn and finally break out. But still, the whole thing had a quality of unreality about it. No one seemed to be shooting at us, but it was getting lighter all the time. Suddenly, a tremendous big blob of yellow light appeared dead ahead; another to the right and another to the left. We were flying straight for them.

Jock pointed out to me the dummy fires and flares to right and left, but we kept going in. Dead ahead there was a whole chain of red flares looking like stoplights. Another Lanc was coned on our starboard beam. The lights seemed to be supporting it. Again we could see those little bubbles of colored lead driving at it from two sides. The German fighters were at him. And then, with no warning at all, D-Dog was filled with an unhealthy white light.

I was standing just behind Jock and could see all the seams on the wings. His quiet Scots voice beat into my ears, "Steady lads, we've been coned." His slender body lifted half out of the seat as he jammed the control column forward and to the left. We were going down. Jock was wearing woolen gloves with the fingers cut off. I could see his fingernails turn white as he gripped the wheel. And then I was on my knees, flat on the deck, for he had whipped the Dog back into a climbing turn. The knees should have been strong enough to support me, but they weren't, and the stomach seemed in some danger of letting me down too. I picked myself up and looked out again. It seemed that one big searchlight, instead of being twenty thousand feet below, was mounted right on our wingtip. D-Dog was corkscrewing. As we rolled down on the other side, I began to see what was happening to Berlin.

Figure 3. Allied planes over Berlin during the bombing in WWII. Date not given, but probably 1943. Photograph. www.the atlantic.com

The clouds were gone, and the sticks of incendiaries from the preceding waves made the place look like a badly laid-out city with the streetlights on. The small incendiaries were going down like a fistful of white rice thrown on a piece of black velvet. As Jock hauled the Dog up again, I was thrown to the other side of the cockpit. And there below were more incendiaries, glowing white and then turning red. The cookies, the four-thousand-pound high explosives, were bursting below like great sunflowers gone mad. And then, as we started down again, still held in the lights, I remembered that the Dog still had one of those cookies and a whole basket of incendiaries in his belly, and the lights still held us, and I was very frightened.

While Jock was flinging us about in the air, he suddenly flung over the intercom, "Two aircraft on the port beam." I looked astern and saw Wally, the mid-upper, whip his turret around to port, and then looked up to see a single-engine fighter slide just above us. The other aircraft was one of ours. Finally, we were out of the cone, flying level. I looked down, and the white fires had turned red. They were beginning to merge and spread, just like butter does on a hot plate. Jock and Buzz, the bomb-aimer, began to discuss the target. The smoke was getting thick down below. Buzz said he liked the two green flares on the ground almost dead ahead. He began calling his directions. And just then a new bunch of big flares went down on the far side of the sea of flame and flare that seemed to be directly below us. He thought that would be a better aiming point. Jock agreed and we flew on.

The bomb doors were opened. Buzz called his directions: "Five left, five left." And then, there was a gentle, confident upward thrust under my feet and Buzz said, "Cookie gone." A few seconds later, the incendiaries went, and D-Dog seemed lighter and easier to handle. I thought I could make out the outline of streets below, but the bomb-aimer didn't agree, and he ought to know. By this time, all those patches of white on black had turned yellow and started to flow together. Another searchlight caught us but didn't hold us. Then, through the intercom came the word, "One can of incendiaries didn't clear. We're still carrying it." And Jock replied, "Is it a big one or a little one?" The word came back: "Little one, I think, but I'm not sure. I'll check." More of those yellow flares came down and hung about us. I haven't seen so much light since the war began.

Figure 4. Race for the Reichstag, Berlin. Battle of Berlin by air, WWII. 1943. Photograph. www.2gravestone.com.

Finally, the intercom announced that it was only a small container of incendiaries left, and Jock remarked, "Well, it's hardly worth going back and doing another run up for that." If there had been a good fat bundle left, he would have gone back through that stuff and done it all over again. I began to breathe, and to reflect again—that all men would be brave if only they could leave their stomachs at home—when there was a tremendous whoomph, an unintelligible shout from the tail gunner, and D-Dog shivered and lost altitude. I looked to the port side and there was a Lancaster that seemed close enough to touch. He had whipped straight under us—missed us by twenty-five, fifty feet, no one knew how much.

The navigator sang out the new course and we were heading for home. And Jock was doing what I had heard him tell his pilots to do so often—flying dead on course. He flew straight into a huge green searchlight, and as he rammed the throttles home remarked, "We'll have a little trouble getting away from this one." And again D-Dog dove, climbed, and twisted, and was finally free. We flew level then. I looked on the port beam at the target area. There was a red, sullen, obscene glare. The fires seemed to have found each other and we were heading home.

For a little while it was smooth sailing. We saw more battles. Then another plane in flames, but no one could tell whether it was ours or theirs. We were still near the target. Dave, the navigator said, "Hold her steady, skipper. I want to get an astral sight." And Jock held her steady. And the flak began coming up at us. It seemed to be very close. It was winking off both wings, but the Dog was steady. Finally, Dave said, "Okay, skipper. Thank you very much." And a great orange blob of flak smacked up straight in front of us, and Jock said, "I think they're shooting at us." I'd thought so for some time. And he began to throw D for Dog up, around, and about again. When we were clear of the barrage, I asked him how close the bursts were and he said, "Not very close. When they're really near, you can smell 'em." That proved nothing for I'd been holding my breath.

Jack sang out from the rear turret, said his oxygen was getting low—thought maybe the lead had frozen. Titch, the wireless operator, went scrambling back with a new mask and a bottle of oxygen. Dave, the navigator, said, "We're crossing the coast." My mind went back to the time I had crossed that coast in 1938, in a plane that had taken off from Prague. Just ahead of me sat two refugees from Vienna—an old man and his wife. The copilot came back and told them that we were outside German territory. The old man reached out and grasped his wife's hand. The work that was done last night was a massive blow of retribution, for all those who have fled from the sound of shots and blows on a stricken continent. We began to lose height over the North Sea. We were over England's shores. The land was dark beneath us. Somewhere down there below, American boys were probably bombing up Fortresses and Liberators, getting ready for the day's work. We were over the home field. We called the control tower and the calm, clear voice of an English girl replied, "Greetings D-Dog. You are diverted to Mulebag." We swung round, contacted Mulebag, came in on the flare path, touched down very gently, ran along to the end of the runway and turned left. And Jock, the finest pilot in Bomber Command, said to the control tower, "D-Dog clear of runway."

When we went in for interrogation, I looked on the board and saw that the big, slow-smiling Canadian and the red-headed English boy with the two-weeks'-old moustache hadn't made it. They were missing.

There were four reporters on this operation. Two of them didn't come back. Two friends of mine, Norman Stockton of Australian Associated Newspapers, and Lowell Bennett, an American representing International News Service. There is something of a tradition amongst reporters, that those who are prevented by circumstances from filing their stories will be covered by their colleagues. This has been my effort to do so. In the aircraft in which I flew, the men who flew and fought it poured into my ears their comments on fighters, flak, and flares in the same tone that they would have used in reporting a host of daffodils. I have no doubt that Bennett and Stockton would have given you a better report of last night's activities.

Figure 5. Edward R. Murrow broadcasting on the radio for CBS. World War II database, WW2db.com.

Berlin was a kind of orchestrated hell—a terrible symphony of light and flame. It isn't a pleasant kind of warfare. The men doing it speak of it as a job. Yesterday afternoon, when the tapes were stretched out on the big map all the way to Berlin and back again, a young pilot with old eyes said to me, "I see we're working again tonight." That's the frame of mind in which the job is being done. The job isn't pleasant; it's terribly tiring. Men die in the sky while others are roasted alive in their cellars. Berlin last night wasn't a pretty sight. In about thirty-five minutes it was hit with about three times the amount of stuff that ever came down on London in a night-long blitz. This is a calculated, remorseless campaign of destruction. Right now the mechanics are probably working on D-Dog, getting him ready to fly again. I return you now to CBS, New York.

CBS Announcer: You have been listening to Edward R. Murrow in an eyewitness report of his experiences in one of the bombers that raided Berlin last night. At 6:45pm, Eastern War Time, Mr. Murrow will again be heard over most of these stations with a report on the highlights of his story. This is the Columbia Broadcasting System.

Figure 6. Edward R. Murrow, reporter, on the streets of London. 1940s. Photograph. Washington State University, wsu.edu.

Postscript by John Barry

As a high school student, on a field trip to Washington, D.C., I noticed Mr. Murrow at the concierge desk across the lobby of the Willard Hotel. He was picking up some theatre tickets, as it turned out, before joining friends for dinner at a nearby restaurant. I know this because I walked over to him and introduced myself. He had left CBS and was then the Director of the United States Information Agency, appointed by President Kennedy two years earlier. There was no mistaking that voice and face, from watching him on TV. I was dazzled by him then, and remain an admirer of his unusual courage and enlightened patriotism even now, most of a lifetime later.

Even when he became world famous, Murrow called himself a 'reporter' or a "newsman," not a 'journalist,' which he thought a self-conscious term.

He grew up in unpretentious surroundings; born in Polecat Creek near Greensboro, North Carolina, grew up in northern Washington state, the son of Quakers, worked in logging camps in the Pacific Northwest, and went to college at Washington State University, majoring in speech.

While a college student, he gave a speech at the annual convention of the National Student Federation of America, an organization that promoted student exchange programs with students of other countries, which resulted in his election as the president of the group. That led to him moving to New York City after graduation. There he worked for the Institute of International Education and the Emergency Committee in Aid of Displaced Foreign Scholars from 1932 to 1935. Murrow led a program that helped displaced German scholars, dismissed from academic positions and persecuted by the Nazis because they were Jewish, find new lives in the United States. Murrow remained on the board of directors of this organization until his death at his home in Pawling, New York in 1965.

By the time he went to work for the Columbia Broadcasting System (CBS) in 1935, Murrow already had first-hand experience with the spreading dangers to free societies presented by one-party states like Hitler's Germany and others. He would go on to witness the German annexation of Austria, the Rhineland, the Sudetenland, Hitler's alliance with Stalin, the joint German-Soviet invasion and destruction of Poland and Western Europe, Germany's attack on England, and finally the German invasion of the Soviet Union, and Japan's attack in the United States in 1941. In his view, the appeasement and isolation practiced by the Western democracies in the 1930s were as much a cause of the Second World War as the imperial ambitions of the Nazi and Japanese dictators. It was for this reason that he reported on the war with such valor and vigor to his American audience.

—J. Barry

---

[1] Columbia Broadcasting System broadcast of December 3, 1943, published as "Reporting World War II, Part One: American Journalism 1938-1944" (The Library of America, 1995), pp. 713-720. The title "Orchestrated Hell" is the title Murrow gave to the report at the time; it also appears in the body of the broadcast.

Bernard Handel's Recollections of World War II

by Candace Lewis (edited)

In 2007, Bernard Handel was video-recorded in an interview about his World War II experiences for the PBS Website (published on September 20, 2007 on YouTube). The interviewer was a New York City professional actor (he did not appear in the interview). In this article, we have reproduced the original interview of 2007 and added a more recent interview of this September, 2019 as an update.

In the years after his service in the U.S. Army during World War II, Bern Handel returned to New York to become an accountant, a specialist in health insurance, pension plans, and retirement plans. He would be one of the consultants who came up with the concept for A.A.R.P. and was involved in its development (1954). Later he would move from New York City to Poughkeepsie, New York and set up the firm The Handel Companies. He is also the founding member of The Handel Foundation, a charitable organization. Although he is semi-retired, Bern claims to one of few 93-year-old fellows who still runs his own company.—C. Lewis, editor

Figure 1. Bernard Handel in his U. S. Army uniform, in Hawaii. 1945. During World War II.

Interview of Bernard Handel in Poughkeepsie, NY September 13, 2019:

C. Lewis: Could you please tell me about how you entered military service in World War II?

B. Handel: That's easy. I was drafted.

C. Lewis: How old were you?

B. Handel: I was eighteen years old.

C. Lewis: What was your life was like at that time?

B. Handel: I was a junior in college, a student at CCNY [City College in New York City]. I was going to school at night and working for the *New York Times* during the day as an unpaid intern—for experience. I wanted to be a newspaper reporter.

At the time, I had two majors, English and Accounting. My English professor at school said it is a terrible idea to be a newspaper man. Be an accountant. So, I was working at the *New York Times*. I got cigarettes, got coffee, did little jobs. The journalists—they were all complaining. They had long hours, lousy pay, no recognition. It made me into an accountant.

More than that, at age 18, I could not tolerate the ultra-conservatism of the *New York Times*. The paper hated FDR. I liked Roosevelt. Oh yeah. All young people did.

Anyway, nobody read the *Times*. My father read the *New York Daily Mirror*. That was in the old days when we had many papers in New York.

C. Lewis: Once you were drafted, what do you remember of your first days and weeks in the Army?

B. Handel: I went first to Fort Dix, then to Camp Blanding in Florida. My most memorable experience was being arrested going into a men's room. It was labeled "Color Only." I thought, what can they do? Arrest me? They did, but the M.P.s bailed me out.

Interview of Bernard Handel in New York City, NY September 20, 2007:

I served in the U.S. Army from the end of 1944 through the end of 1946. I served in Hawaii, and in Okinawa, and in various places preparing for the invasion of Japan. And after the war, I served in the Office of the Commanding General Pacific Ocean areas in connection with Ordnance, registration, relocation, and reshipment back to the United States. Originally, I was supposed to go into the Army Specialized Training Program in the Air Force. Because of the casualties suffered in the Battle of the Bulge, there was a sudden demand for troops, or would-be troops.

I was a full-time employee, going to college part-time. I was in my sophomore year. And when you reached 18, you were drafted. You were—it was conscription. There was no choice. The original decision—my original choice—was to go into what was ASTB, which was a program where you actually went back to college as a [pause] while you were in the Army. I was supposed to be sent to the University of Delaware and then, suddenly, the Battle of the Bulge changed all that and they eliminated all the specialized training programs that was leading to specialist and put everybody into the infantry.

And I went to Camp Blanding in Florida and I was rushed into the very efficient basic training which, in 12 to 15 weeks, really produced. It remarkably changed all of us. And I and all my fellow soldiers really became very efficient and trained. And for a city boy who had never fired a gun in my life, I was amazed how efficient they were in training everybody and making us into people possibly capable of fighting a war.

Because I was a college junior and I was thrown in with a bunch of eighteen-year-old kids who came from all over the country, I became sort of the Cyrano de Bergerac of many of the kids from the South, and Appalachia, and other areas. I became their consultant by writing their love letters to their lady friends. This had some advantages. Since I was a city guy, who had no real experience as an outdoorsman—who was not very handy—I needed help in things like assembling a rifle, a machine gun, and building a tent, building a foxhole. My talents as a literary author or co-author of their letters came in very handy in barter for all the services I received in helping me. And I must say that many of these people were tremendously nice, and helpful, and courteous. And the amount of assistance that people gave each other was always impressive in the Army.

Once we completed our training in Florida, we were sent to Fort Camp Rucker in Alabama as a group. They probably were going to arrange to have us sent to Europe but the war in Europe came to an end. So suddenly, we were redeployed. After a short visit home, we redeployed and went on a rather weird 12-day meandering railroad trip across the United States to

Seattle. We were then, after this long trip—and we stayed in Seattle at Fort Lawton for a while until they then put us on a troop ship. We set a meandering zig-zag path across the Pacific over eight days to Hawaii. In Hawaii, we were all assigned as infantry replacements. We went to Schofield Barracks and started to undergo very vigorous training in jungle training and fighting in the war in the Pacific. This was after we had been through village training for a war in Europe. So it was a major change in the training policy.

And so then we were reassigned after that as infantry replacements. We were shipped to various islands in the Pacific. I ended up in the last stages of the war in Okinawa. I was very fortunate in that the war came to an end in Okinawa. So we had very little combat experience.

Then we started going on a long training period for what would be the invasion of Japan.

One of the humorous things was the fact that everybody knew of a certain date, which was November first. If there was going to be a major invasion, it was certainly the worst kept secret in history, whether that date was correct or not.

We went on numerous amphibious landings preparing for battles in the Japanese mainland. No one looked forward to the war in the Japan mainland, based upon the vigorous battles put up by the Japanese in Iwo Jima and Okinawa with the huge American casualties, as well as the tremendous civilian casualties in Okinawa.

We were doing a landing on August 6th, 1945, one of our part dry landings, which were very difficult because of the heat, and getting water in your boots, and making numerous landings on the same day. And suddenly, one of my—one of the other soldiers said to me, hey, Joe College—because I was the only college man, I completed two years of college, in the group. What do you know about the dropping of a bomb? Could you make a bomb out of atoms? Having taken physics in college, I nonchalantly said, don't kid yourself; there's no such thing. It's impossible. It never can happen. One of my clear memories of the war and everybody believed me.

Then when we got back that night, the story had been told that the United States had dropped an atomic on Hiroshima and, of course, that led a week later, after the bombing of Nagasaki, to the end of the war. Many of us, including myself, firmly believed that most of us owe our lives to the fact that we never had to invade Japan and the war came to an end after the dropping of the atomic bomb. We think Truman was a great guy for making that decision.

Well, after the war ended, they suddenly started to determine what they would do with us. They were going to redeploy many people that served many years overseas back home and they went through our specialties. I was assigned, based on my accounting background and office background, to the Office of the Commanding General in Ordnance and ended up in a fantastic interesting job for over a year in finding out where American war equipment was in the Pacific; locating it; inventorying it; and determining what should be shipped back; what we declared surplus; and what would be abandoned as war losses.

Other than the short period of being constantly afraid of getting killed in combat, and I was fortunate in that respect, I would say you come away from military training with an unbelievably high opinion of the operational capacity of the U.S. Army to develop troops, to turn citizens into fighting men, their professionalism, their discipline, and the way they train people, and the high level of professionalism they display in all their capacities.

The U.S. Armed Forces are maligned very frequently. However, we did not see that. When I was in the Army, I had a high opinion of the officers and the enlisted men. I ended up a sergeant. I thought most of the people I met were very efficient, and very professional, and did a great job. I think the great experience of the war is all the people you meet, the people you —the gentlemen that you dealt with, how fine they were, the comraderie that developed. People really did work together of all types, despite their backgrounds and they all had a common cause.

The Second World War furnished that cause. Most people had a high opinion of the reasons for the war. I think that is the major difference between the Vietnamese War and the War in Iraq today is that many people question whether we should have been in those wars and the extent to which we were in the wars.

The other thing, of course, the major difference between certainly the Iraq War at the present time and the Second World War, everyone in the Second World War was involved. Conscription took everybody of all ages, all people. There was no choice. It was a citizen Army. Whether that's good or bad is something else but they were citizens who received unbelievably professional, quick training which changed them from being laymen into professional soldiers in an unbelievably short period of time. I don't think that could happen again today because the technology involved in warfare today would make it impossible to really use citizen soldiers in the same way. I think it probably requires a year or two of training today to produce a soldier who could fight under today's conditions. But I think those are the major changes that have occurred since the Second World War.

After the War, we lost a lot of friends because, under the GI Bill, people did not go back to their original schools. They went many places. It was hard to keep track of people. I have some people---friends---I remember, I knew afterwards but only a few. And I must say we have kept in contact over the years.

Interview of Bernard Handel in Poughkeepsie, NY September 13, 2019:

C. Lewis: It is now several years since your interview in 2007. It is now 2019, a long time away from the events of the 1940s. As you reflect again on your time in the service, do you have any comments?

B. Handel: The American soldier was loved. He gave candy to children; he gave cigarettes to civilians. He freed populations from servitude. We have lost that. We were respected.

Another thing. The Second World War was won by civilians. The best were citizens who had had other experiences in their backgrounds. They brought these experiences and training to their service in the military. They worked hard. I wonder about that now.

Are the people the best for the military now? Now we do not have the draft. Of course, the all volunteer army has its advantages. And the disadvantages are obvious. Of course everyone would be on the government payroll if we had the draft. Everyone could go to V.A. hospitals forever.

C. **Lewis**: Any other thoughts about World War II?

B. Handel: For those that survived it, World War II was the experience of our lives—of my life. Going to different countries, meeting people from all over our country, getting along with all kinds of people. This was terrific. No one really cared about your political views. People were really patriotic.

[1] https://www.youtube.com/watch?v=N8YLJA8xuls8xuls&t=158s. The proceedings of this interview have been electronically recorded for the Dutchess County Historical Society and a transcript produced by Kimberly J. Zogby of American Legal Transcription, Poughkeepsie, NY 12601. We would like to express our gratitude to Mary Kate Babiarz, the leader of that organization.

The Fighting O'Connells: Twentieth-Century American Soldiers

by Candace J. Lewis

Joan O'Connell Smith says that the fighting spirit runs deep and wide in her family. Her grandfather fought in World War I; her father served in World War II; and her two older brothers served in the Vietnam War. This is the story of those four men. It is pieced together from personal memories and a family archive, a somewhat uneven narrative. But, wait, says Joan: you should know that this spirit comes from the forebears of the O'Connells and from our other ancestors—of the Haynes family, from long ago. This is not just a twentieth-century phenomenon.

According to family tradition, in the time just before the outbreak of the American Revolution, great-great grand-uncle Deacon Josiah Haynes was living in Sudbury, in the vicinity of Concord, Massachusetts. When he heard of the advance of the redcoats from Boston towards Lexington and Concord on that fateful day in April 1775, he grabbed his gun and walked eight miles through the night to join the fight. As he arrived in Concord, he was met by the head of the local militia. Apparently, this local commander was advocating caution. We have recorded the actual words of old Josiah Haynes. He replied: "If you don't go and drive them British from that bridge, I shall call you a coward."[1]

And he was no youngster spoiling for a fight, and full of the ideals of liberty. He was an old guy. At that moment, Mr. Haynes was 79 years old. In the O'Connell family, says his descendant Joan Smith of her family members, "When there is a fight, they are going to be there. They can't seem to help themselves."

Grandfather: Raymond G. O'Connell "Ray": Served in World War I

Raymond G. O'Connell was born in Cold Spring, New York on October 1, 1884. He died not far away in Fishkill, New York of October 4, 1951. He enlisted in the military for World War I on December 6, 1917 (SVN 2505506). The opening of the draft in Dutchess County had begun in April

Figure 1. Grandfather: Corporal Raymond G. O'Connell "Ray" who fought in World War I. Member of Company "K," the 23rd Engineers. 1917-1919. Grandfather of Joan O'Connell Smith. Photograph. Collection of Joan O'Connell Smith.

1917. He joined a few months later. He served as a corporal in Company "K," the 23rd Engineers, and was discharged on June 17, 1919 (Figure 1).

His service included stints at Camp Mead, Camp Laurel, Camp Glen Burnie to Hoboken, transport from Fort George Washington to France. He also saw duty at Brest, Genecort, St. Sulpice, Chaumont G.H.Q., Dombask, and the Meuse-Argonne battle front. He would have witnessed and participated in some of the worse battles of the war. As far as we know, Raymond never told stories of his time at these difficult battlefields—that is, not to immediate family and friends. He was, however, clearly proud of his service.

The 23rd Engineers Regiment (Road) was formed as part of the 3rd Armored Division of the US Army on August 15, 1917. In a mere three weeks, the unit was able to gather together a number of men and activate the regiment at Camp Meade, Maryland. We believe Raymond would have been a part of this initial group. The 23rd Engineers began deploying to France very quickly—in November 1917. They were called "The Road Builders of the AEF," building and rebuilding roads and bridges for the main and support troops of the Army.

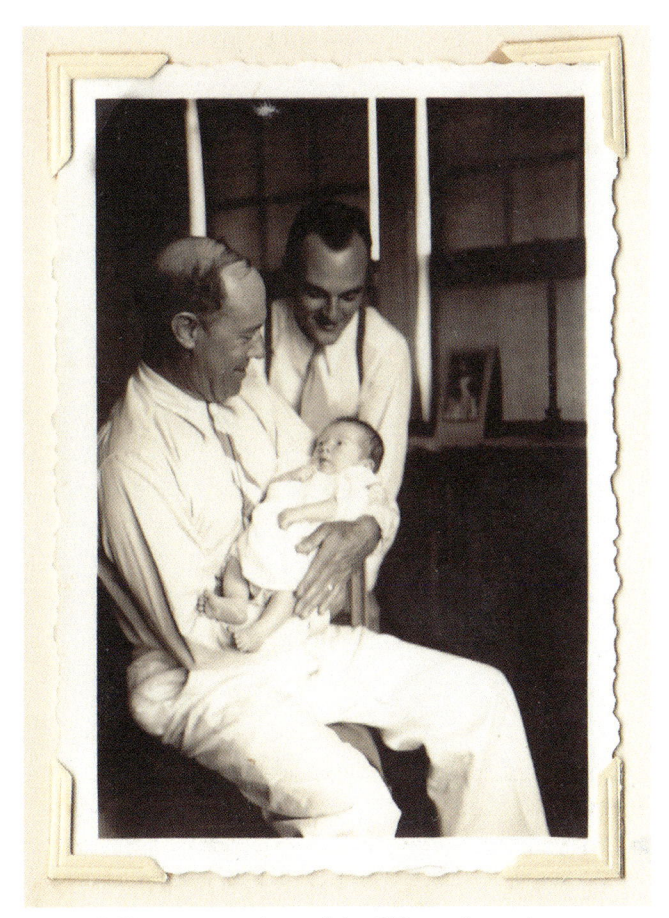

Figure 2. Three generations of the O'Connell men in 1939 with the birth of baby Ray. Grandfather Raymond G. O'Connell, father Bernard Joseph O'Connell, Sr., and baby Raymond Sheldon O'Connell, one month old. Photograph. Collection of Joan O'Connell Smith.

From the time of the surrender of the German Army until June 1919, the 23rd Engineers continued their work of clean-up and repair in Europe. They were demobilized on June 16, 1919 at Camp Deven, Massachusetts. This date accords exactly with the record of Raymond's service. He finished his service on June 17, 1919.

When he returned home to the Hudson Valley, he took up residence in the Hudson Valley, first in Cold Spring, later in Fishkill. He became an engineer, working building roads. He would do this for the remainder of his career. During one period after the war, Raymond was living with his family in Cold Spring, New York in a little house a couple of blocks from the Hudson River. He had his son, Bernie, who was then 10 or 12 years old, pull out the row boat, put in their small dog and row his dad across the river to work early in the morning. (This would have been happening around 1927 to 1929.) Raymond would work all day as an engineer on the construction of the Storm King Mountain Highway and then get into the row boat with his young son at the end of the day to return home across the river. This method, presumably, was much easier and cheaper than going to the ferry crossing in Beacon several miles up the river.

Joan Smith has a strong memory of Ray, her grandfather. Grandfather Ray died a couple of weeks before Joan's fifth birthday. Joan and her family were in Fishkill with Grandpa and his wife. He was probably quite frail at the time. It would have been 1951. He gave his little granddaughter a stuffed dog (Figure 3). She still has it and treasures it. All over the dog were affixed the medals that Ray had been awarded for his service and bravery in "The War." Unfortunately, the medals are now gone.

Figure 3. The Stuffed dog that Ray O'Connell gave to his five-year-old granddaughter, Joan, in 1951. When he gave it to her, it was covered with his World War I medals, but his wife asked to retain them for a later date when the child would be older. Unfortunately, no one in the family has been able to locate the medals. Photograph by Candace Lewis.

Father: Bernard Joseph O'Connell, Sr. "Bernie": served in World War II

Raymond's son, Bernard Joseph O'Connell, Sr., "Bernie," was born in Poughkeepsie, New York at Saint Francis Hospital on March 28, 1917. He was born in the year his own father departed for *his* war—World War I, the "war to end all wars," and would grow up to serve in the next great conflagration, World War II (Figure 4). He would die in 2000 in Poughkeepsie, New York at Vassar Hospital and be buried at the Rural Cemetery.

Figure 4. Father: Bernard Joseph O'Connell, Sr. "Bernie." Father of Joan O'Connell Smith. Served in World War II. Photograph. Collection of Joan O'Connell Smith.

Military service must have stood as a shining beacon in the O'Connell family, because well before the beginning of World War II, Bernie was already a soldier. It was the period of the Depression in the United States and times could not have been easy, but one suspects that Bernie's motivation for enlisting in the 1930s may not have been entirely monetary. He may have been attracted by his father's pride in his own service years before, during World War I. Also in 1935, the army would have offered steady work, training, and an opportunity to travel beyond the Hudson Valley. He would have been a very young man, only eighteen years old, when he enlisted. Judging by the larger amount of material in the family archive relating to this early service in the army, it would appear that this period was the more influential in the life of the young man—more important, perhaps, than his service during World War II.

Bernie was assigned to Company A, 27th Infantry and was stationed at Schofield Barracks in Hawaii, near Pearl Harbor from 1935 to 1937 (Figure 5), well before the 1941 devastating attack on Pearl Harbor. We have evidence that Bernie was in Hawaii by October of that fall, because he kept a certificate attesting to the fact that he had climbed the volcano Hui O Pele Hawaii on Oct 25, 1935.

Figure 5. Schofied Barracks near Pearl Harbor, Hawaii. 1935. Bernie O'Connell was stationed here during his first stint in the army, 1935-1937. Photograph. Collection of Joan O'Connell Smith.

Bernie loved sports and, while in the army, he coached sports teams. He was called a "trainer." It seems a particular interest was the boxing team. At the beginning of December 1935, Bernie sent his mother a Christmas card from Hawaii (Figure 6). Inside he enclosed a tissue-thin map of the northern island of Luzon in the archipelago of the Phillipines (Figure 7). Apparently, the army boxing team had visited the area (Figure 8).

Also, when he was stationed at Schofield Barracks in Hawaii, he and his team were planning to go to South East Asia and China for a boxing tournament, but they were forced to cancel the trip because the Japanese invaded Manchuria in northeastern China (1936).

Figure 6. Christmas card sent by Bernie O'Connell from Hawaii to his mother in Poughkeepsie in December 1935. Collection of Joan O'Connell Smith.

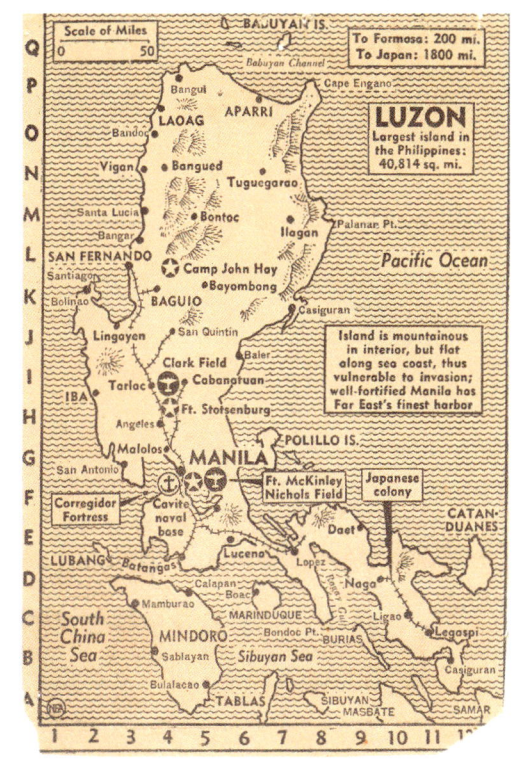

Figure 7. Map of Luzon enclosed with the Christmas card sent by Bernie to his mother in December 1935. Collection of Joan O'Connell Smith.

Figure 8. Boxing team from Fort Slocum, Hawaii, 1935. Photograph. On reverse is written: Boxing Team, Fort Slocum, 1935. Team: Wallace R. Berger-Heavyweight; Vernon Eaves-middle"; Henry Fright-Heavy"; Bernard O'Connell-Light"/Championship Recruiting team, Hawaii. (Joan has identified Bernie as young man standing, second from left.) Photograph. Collection of Joan O'Connell Smith.

Figure 9. Bernie, who was known as "Duke" for his resemblance to the movie star, John Wayne. He is standing in front of his tent at Schofield Barracks, Hawaii, 1937. Photograph. Collection of Joan O'Connell Smith.

On July 14, 1937, Bernie sent a telegram to his mother saying that he had reached San Francisco and was "Leaving tonight for Los Angeles. Will wire departure from there. Having fine trip. Feeling fine. Bernard." The photo of the Army transport ship *Republic* with a penciled date "'37" suggests that Bernie traveled from Hawaii to San Francisco on this vessel at the end of his service (Figure 10).

Figure 10. US Army Transport *Republic*. Ship that took Bernie O'Connell from Hawaii to San Francisco at the end of his service in July 1937. Photograph. Collection of Joan O'Connell Smith.

After this, he returned to Poughkeepsie. It appears that he had left the Army, his term up. Then World War II started for the United States with Pearl Harbor in December 1941. Soldiers, sailors, and airmen were mustered for another great war. Two years later, in 1943, Bernie would sign up to serve again. At this time, he would have been 26 years old, a young husband, father, with a job in Dutchess County. Soon thereafter he again went to Camp Crowder in Missouri.

Father Raymond O'Connell and his second wife, Doll, wrote to son Bernie on December 1, 1943 (spelling not changed):

Dear Son,

Rec'd your letter from Camp Crowder yesterday Nov. 30, and Doll [Bernie's stepmother] and I were surely supprised. Thought you would have a longer stay at Upton, but you can never tell what the army will do. I can imagine how you were cramped in coaches and so little to eat, which reminds me how we were over crowded in box cars for three days going to front in 1917 in France. You were lucky to get to Camp Crowder in time for your Thanksgiving dinner and after reading the Menu you sent I know you all had a fine dinner and plenty of everything. Now son, put everything in your 6-weeks Basic training and get the best marks you know how, so you can go to a spec. training school, as I know it will be very Interesting and a big help to you in yr's. to come.

Don't worry about being shipped oversea's just yet, as you will have to get your proper training first. Don't forget to drop a line when you have time, even if it is only a postal.

I surely would like to see your camp of 65,000 troops. I understand that Missouri has more Army camps then any other state; from what you state in your letter it must be mostly for Engineers.

Good by for now and don't delay in dropping a line.

Good luck and Good health.

From

Doll & Dad

Figure 11. Treasury Department Buddy Bond purchased by Mrs. Ruth O'Connell (Bernie's wife) in honor of Corporal Bernard O'Connell, Co. C, 28 B n, 6th Reg, Camp Crowder, Missouri. "We are all backing the attack with 'Buddy Bonds.'" Fourth War Loan: Jan 18 to Feb 15, 1944. Dutchess County Buddy Honor Roll. John E. Mack, Honorary County Chairman. Collection of Joan O'Connell Smith.

Again, as in his previous service of the 1930s, Bernie was scheduled to go overseas. However, he had to come back here to Poughkeepsie because his mother-in-law died. During the visit, Bernie was swinging his younger son, Joe, on the swing set and he injured his left eye. He was never able to see out of that eye again. He was able to continue to serve, but not overseas. Thus, throughout World War II, Bernie was stationed at Fort Crowder in Missouri doing cryptanalysis and coaching and training of the boxing team (Figure 12).

Figure 12. Father: Sergeant Bernie O'Connell at Camp Crowder in Missouri with all the other soldiers, 1945. He is the man at the front with no hat. He was the trainer. This unit was the rifle champs and softball champs. Photograph. Collection of Joan O'Connell Smith.

When Bernie came home from his service in World War II in 1947, he took a job at Hudson River State Hospital. He started as a telephone operator, then worked as an attendant, and was promoted to the position of nurse in the 1950s. He retired in the 1970s. In addition, after the war, Bernie developed a second job for himself. He was a bookkeeper, free-lance, working for smaller local companies. He never wanted to sign on with a CPA firm, because he valued his independence. He also valued the extra income for his family and the relationships he gained through his work. Finally, another aspect of his post-war life was his service in the army reserves. In the summers, Bernie would go to stay at Camp Wellfleet in Massachusetts for training (Figures 13 and 14). Clearly, his years of military service were supremely important to him.

Figure 13. Bernie and troops at Camp Wellfleet, Massachusetts for summer training of Army Reserves. C. 1950s. Sergeant Bernard O'Connell is at the front in crouching position. Photograph. Collection of Joan O'Connell Smith.

Figure 14. Bernard J. O'Connell as a member of the Army Reserves. Shown here with Army officers pointing to a map of Hawaii. They are at Summer Camp, Camp Wellfleet, Massachusetts. Date not certain, perhaps about 1960. Photograph. Collection of Joan O'Connell Smith.

Letters to Bernie

Bernard Joseph O'Connell, Sr. served in World War II

We don't have any letters or speeches from Bernie, but we can gain considerable insight into his way of thinking from the letters of a good friend he made during World War II. This was a British friend who was a member of the Royal Marines, a corporal, M. G. Taylor, known as "Buck." He hailed from the little town of Whitenap in Romsey, England.—C. Lewis, editor

Following are excerpts from letters written by Buck Taylor to Bernie in 1990 and 1991 (spelling has been left unchanged):

From Pieter Maritzburg, Republic of South Africa, August, 1990

> ...Sometimes I wonder what it's all about Bernie: I reckon we think much the same as each other—like for instance it may be old-fashioned but on TV the other night we watched some hooligans burning the US flag and were so upset. You'll probably be the first to agree that 'Yanks' blow their own trumpets and enjoy their 'ballyhoo', but their pride is something worthwhile: I know that there's a certain attraction and deep feeling they have for their country that just comes naturally to them. Even foreigners sense it, part of their way, life itself. It's that if you like patriotism we all one knew....

From England: March 15, 1991

> ...Bernie, I've often wondered about your thoughts on the Gulf War now behind us? For me, thank God it was solved so quickly with such a remarkable few men on our side lost. I loathe the thought of anyone dying in wartime, especially because of some maniac like S. Hussien, but he brought the destruction on people and country. He had all the warning any fool could expect. The U. N. won the "Mother of all battles," the States bearing the brunt of it all, but I really do believe that other fools have now had it proved to them that it's not worth while defying world opinion. I somehow think that in the long run, other countries in that area (and others) will profit by it e.g. Israel & Arabs! With all my heart I thank the States for

their share in winning as they did. Tragedy for so many of your country's people, somewhat fewer for U.K. but without the technology used it might well have resulted in thousands more deaths all round.

You might think it's old-fashioned to think as I do, but I don't believe it is so. Like 1939's war, I felt it was a just war. I reckon you do too. I share in your pride of the Stars & Stripes, the terrific efficiency and keenness, the staggering armaments available and ability to get them where wanted. The organization was a marvel, and the leadership top class. For the Britishers also, the low-level bombing and tanks (what A1 machines they are), the mine-sweeping etc of the navy and general clearing up! I'll bet you were also a bit puffed up with it all. Make no mistake Bernie, I detest war and any violence—but am capable of admiration for those having to do the dirty work. I'm not a 'Yank,' but by God I'm thankful to be capable of sharing in your country's pride....

The Two sons: Raymond Sheldon O'Connell "Ray," and Bernard Joseph O'Connell, Jr. "Joe": both served during the Vietnam War

Information about sons Ray and Joe (Figure 15) is not abundant; both served in the military during the Vietnam War of the 1960s and early 1970s. Neither of these men was eager to relive and relate the experiences of those years. This is a brief sketch.

Raymond Sheldon O'Connell, "Ray," served in the US Navy during the Vietnam War. He was born on May 15, 1939 at Vassar Hospital in Poughkeepsie, New York where he grew up and when to local public schools.

Figure 15. The Two sons: Raymond Sheldon O'Connell "Ray," and Bernard Joseph O'Connell, Jr. "Joe": both served in the Vietnam War. Here they are shown as small boys. Photograph. Collection of Joan O'Connell Smith.

Ray served on the USS Forrestal (CVA-59) from February 1, 1962 into 1965. He sailed the Atlantic and Pacific Oceans and the Mediterranean Sea. He spent some of his time during the Vietnam War on the aircraft carrier traveling around Southeast Asia. As a member of Division V-2, Unit AAG, he was trained to launch and recover aircraft on the flight deck of the enormous vessel. He and the team he belonged to operated catapults, arresting gears, and visual landing aids (Figures 16, 17, and 18).

According to his sister, Joan, Ray doesn't like to talk about his experiences during this time. One story he told her was about his best friend on board USS Forrestal, a fellow sailor from Long Island. One day, Ray was ill and couldn't go up on deck to work on the landing planes and the catapults. His friend took his place. A bad accident followed with a plane landing and his friend was killed. A few years later, when Ray was getting married, the deceased friend's parents and his brother attended the wedding. Ray was very moved by their continuing concern for him, a concern that was mutual.

Figure 16. *USS Forrestal*, CVA-59. United States Navy aircraft carrier. The ship was 1,039 feet long, 252 feet wide, 25 stories high. Usually had 4,200 servicemen on board. It carried the following aircraft: Skywarrior, Skyhawk, Skyraider, Tracer, Phantom II, Crusader, Trader, and SH 3A (helo). Photograph from a Navy brochure. N.d. (after the Vietnam War). Collection of Joan O'Connell Smith.

Figure 17. Aircraft on board the *USS Forrestal*, CV A-59. United States Navy aircraft carrier. Photograph from a Navy brochure. N.d. (after the Vietnam War). Collection of Joan O'Connell Smith.

Figure 18. Aircraft on board the *USS Forrestal*, CV A-59. United States Navy aircraft carrier. Photograph from a Navy brochure. N.d. (after the Vietnam War). Collection of Joan O'Connell Smith.

He left the Navy after the Vietnam War, but stayed in the reserves until the late 1990s. Ray now lives in Boynton Beach, Florida.

Younger brother, Bernard Joseph O'Connell, Jr., "Joe," also served in the US Navy during the Vietnam War. He was born at Vassar Brothers Hospital, on June 25, 1940, in the year after his older brother, Ray. He was brought up in Poughkeepsie and attended schools here before entering the Navy. During the period of the Vietnam War, he went on two deployments in the Seabees. Later he went directly to Antarctica where he continued in service. He retired from the Seabees in the 1990s.

Conclusion

Thus, four members of the O'Connell family have served in the US Armed Forces in major conflicts of the twentieth century. The grandfather, Raymond O'Connell, was in the engineer corps serving in Europe during World War I; and father, Bernie O'Connell, was a sergeant training troops in Missouri during World War II. Both looked upon their years of military service with pride. While they were not always forthcoming with accounts of their times in service, at least to family and friends who had not shared in the experience, they remained closely connected to the army through the reserves. They had been in the wars that were massively supported by a broad spectrum of the military, the political establishment, and the entire populace at home.

The two brothers, Joe and Ray O'Connell, who served during the Vietnam War of the 1960s and 1970s, were extremely reluctant to relate the stories of their service. They, unlike their father and grandfather, served during a time of fractious political upheaval at home about their conflict. Support for their efforts was often meager. We should note that it is often thought that the reluctance of veterans to speak of the Vietnam War was due to the particular violence that the men experienced. It would appear, however, that violence could be horrific in any of the wars of the twentieth century and often affected veterans deeply. The factor that was different for the Vietnam War was the lack of support for the fight by the whole population at home. In this account, as in many others, we see a marked reluctance of veterans to share detailed stories of their military encounters with folks who have not shared their experiences. What they have been willing to share, however, has been their pride in their service and their country.

The spirit of service has continued in the O'Connell family in the end of the twentieth century and the beginning of the twenty-first. Joan O'Connell Smith served in the Red Cross at a military hospital in southern California. Her younger son, Jimmy, is not in the military, but he is a volunteer fireman. The warrior spirit too lives on. Even today, Joan's older son, Bill, a graduate of Annapolis, is serving as a Commander in the US Navy.

---

[1] A.J. Langguth, *Patriots: The Men Who Started the American Revolution* (New York, London: Simon and Schuster, 1988), p. 246.

[2] See "The 23rd Engineers in World War I: 'Road Builders of the AEF'" in http://www.3ad.org/unit-web-sites/23d-engineer-battalion/world-war-1/

ARTICLES

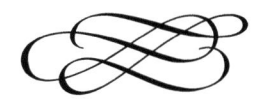

The Clarks of Nagaland

by Elizabeth C. Strauss

Who would think that Amenia, New York, would be a place of pilgrimage for people from Nagaland, India? Where is Nagaland? That's what I wondered after receiving an email from a woman named Narola in August of 2014. Narola Ao McFayden Ph.D. and her husband Kenneth McFayden were planning to drive from Virginia to Amenia, in order to visit the graves of Rev. Edward Clark and his wife, Mrs. Mary Mead Clark.

Figure 1. Nagaland is an eastern province of India, northeast of Bangladesh and north of Myanmar.

Introduction

The Clarks were a missionary couple who traveled to India over 150 years ago and devoted 42 years of their lives to service in that distant land. Their influence upon the people of Nagaland, India, is still appreciated today. Their names are revered, and their contributions have been memorialized. Consequently, their resting place, the Amenia Island Cemetery in Amenia, New York, is considered to be sacred ground.

When Narola and Ken arrived in Amenia later in the month of August 2014, I was able to give them a tour of where Edward Clark and Mary Mead had grown up, showing them their homes and schools and churches. When we were at the cemetery, Narola placed flowers on the graves, took photographs, and then made a phone call. She explained later that she had called her relatives in Nagaland to tell them that she was finally at the Clarks' gravesite. In her quiet, gentle voice she told us that they had responded with tears of amazement and joy.

Nagaland is little known here in America. It is an ancient state of India, regarded as part of the province of Assam until 1961, when it became a state of the modern nation—a small, mountainous area in the far eastern part of the country, east of the contemporary country Bangladesh, and bordering on Myanmar.

Figure 2. Narola Ao McFayden, Ph.D. and Ken McFayden at the graves of Edward W. and Mary Mead Clark, Amenia Island Cemetery, Amenia, NY. The gravestone of the Clark's only child, Carrie, is lying on the ground at right and has since been repaired. Photo by E.C. Strauss, 2014.

The Early Life of the Clarks in Dutchess County, New York and their Education

Edward Winter Clark was born in 1830 in the Town of North East. His father passed away when he was eight years old. Edward remained on the family farm with his mother and two siblings until he left for Worcester Academy in Massachusetts in his teen years. Edward went on to Brown University in Providence, Rhode Island for higher education and graduated in 1857. After a year of study at Newton Theological Seminary in Massachusetts and before completing a year at Rochester Theological Seminary in Rochester, New York he married Miss Mary Mead.

Figure 3. Mrs. Mary Mead Clark, 1832-1924, Rev. Edward Winter Clark, 1830-1913. Photos Collection of the North East Historical Society.

Mary Jane Mead was born in 1832 in the Town of Amenia. She attended the one-room schoolhouse in her neighborhood, before continuing her education at Amenia Seminary. Just how or when Mary met Edward Clark is not known, but since both of their families were active in the Baptist churches of their respective towns, Amenia and North East, it is likely that introductions were made through the churches.

It is important to note that the Amenia Seminary, founded in 1835, had a reputation for inspiring, within its students, scholarly excellence and a commitment to God by serving others. Established by Methodist scholars connected with Wesleyan University in Middletown, Connecticut, Amenia Seminary was a coeducational boarding school, which attracted students from many states and foreign countries. Many of its graduates went on to become professors and college presidents, lawyers and judges, military leaders, ministers, and, as in the case of Mary Mead, missionaries to distant lands.[1]

At the Amenia Seminary Reunion of 1906, Mrs. Mary Mead Clark was the only female alumna asked to give an address. At that time, Mrs. Clark was in her 70s, home on furlough, and soon to retire from mission work. One would assume that her talk would have been about her extraordinary adventures and accomplishments. However, she simply shared happy memories of student life and spoke of the inspiration she had gained while at Amenia Seminary.[2]

Worcester Academy, where Edward received his secondary education, was founded in 1834 as the "Worcester County Manual Labor High School." It was a day and boarding school which offered courses in academics as well as vocational skills, such as the use of the printing press. No doubt, this is where Edward acquired his printing press training, as well as training in construction and engineering, which he put to good use years later in India.

Figure 4. Printing Press Wheel in Clark Museum in Molungyimsen. Photo by Imyangerla Aier. Photo. Collection of Narola Ao McFayden and Kenneth McFayden.

Edward W. Clark and Mary Mead were married in Amenia on September 29, 1858 by the Rev. Thomas Vassar of the Amenia Baptist Church. Upon completion of his ministerial training in 1859, Edward received his first assignment as an ordained minister in Logansport, Indiana. There he served as pastor for just two years.

Over the next several years, Edward and Mary remained affiliated with the Logansport Baptist Church, but took on a new work in Indianapolis, Indiana editing a magazine called *The Witness*.

During this time, they were approached by the American Baptist Foreign Mission Society with an invitation to serve in Assam, India printing religious and educational material for the mission schools there. The Clarks were willing and eager to take the assignment, but the loss of their only child at almost four years of age and Mary's poor health held them back until the autumn of 1868.

Travel to India

Thus, Edward and Mary Clark left their homeland October 20, 1868. The journey to India took 160 days, more than five months aboard a Boston trading vessel, the bark *Pearl*. They were bound for Calcutta, via the Cape of Good Hope.[3]

According to Mary Mead's book, *A Corner in India*, they sailed the entire trip without putting in at any port and without sighting land.

Mary wrote about the storms at sea, about all the passengers learning to navigate the ship, because there was nothing else to do, about the drinking water turning to slime, and about the food getting wormy. When they arrived in Calcutta, the stalwart couple still had to endure a two-week journey, traveling by railroad for a few hours, then 14 days by steamboat up the Brahmaputra River, then a few hours by elephant, an overnight trip on a dugout canoe type of raft, powered by native men poling against the riverbank, and finally the last eight miles by ponies, to the mission station. They arrived in Assam in March of 1869.[4]

During their early years at the mission station at Sibsagor, Rev. Clark worked in the printing shop, printing scriptures and school books in the Assamese language. Mary taught young women in the mission school. While busy with their work, the Clarks often heard the pounding of the log drums from up in the Naga Hills. Rev. Clark was feeling a desire to communicate with the remote tribal people who beat the drums. The Naga warriors were headhunters. According to Mrs. Clark's written account, the men collected the skulls of those they killed and stored them in skull houses in their villages. They reasoned that the more skulls they had, the more the neighboring tribes would fear them.[5]

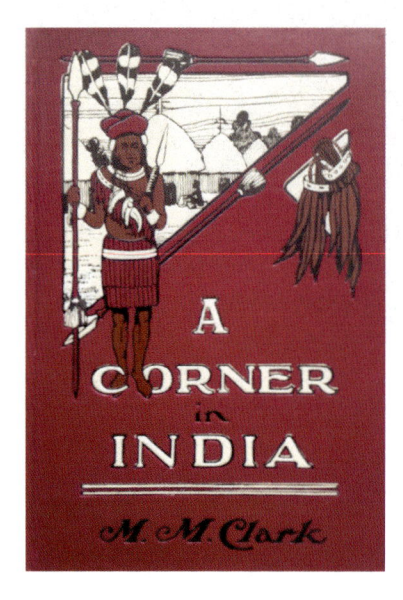

Figure 5. Book by Mary Mead Clark, *A Corner in India*, published 1906. Photo by E.C. Strauss.

The Naga people were superstitious and lived in constant fear. Of course, there were many things to be afraid of: sudden raids by neighboring tribes, being attacked by wild animals, like tigers and snakes, epidemic diseases and death. They believed that the many spirits of the earth and sky had to be appeased with sacrifices in order for them to be safe and healthy.

Rev. Clark Devises a Plan to Become Missionary to the Headhunters

Occasionally, Naga men would come down from their mountain villages to the tea plantations of Assam to buy salt. They observed the schools at the mission station and expressed an interest in having their own children learn to read. Rev. Clark's heart went out to them. He wanted to befriend the Naga people. The Mission Board back in the States was reluctant to let Edward Clark go to a place where he would be in danger. Nevertheless, Clark devised a plan.

Figure 6. A Naga Spear now in the possession of Edward Clark's grand-nephew who lives in the Town of North East. Photo by E. C. Strauss.

There was an Assamese man who had become a Christian through the witness of a missionary who was there before the Clarks. This Assamese man, like Rev. Clark, wanted to reach out to the Naga people. The man's name was Godhula. Fortunately, the Mission Board agreed to let Godhula go up to one of the Naga villages to determine if there was any receptivity to the Bible message. This was in October of 1871. When Godhula went to the village of Dekha Haimong, he was immediately locked up in a small hut. The leaders of the village suspected that he was working as a spy for the British government or for the East Indies Company. They gave him very little to eat and just watched him. In a simple and unassuming way, Godhula began to sing songs and hymns. Because the people were curious and liked the music, they came near and listened to the songs. They were attracted to Godhula and began to listen to his stories. After about a week, Godhula was released. He returned to Rev. Clark with encouraging news. The following spring, 1872, Godhula and his wife Lucy went up to the village of Dekha Haimong again and stayed until November. When they returned to Rev. Clark in November, they brought with them nine converts to be baptized.[6]

A few days later, Rev. Edward Clark went with these nine people back to the village. He stayed with them for a week, after which time, on December 23, 1872, fifteen more converts confessed their new faith and desired to be baptized. This was the beginning of the church in Nagaland.

The mission board in America still would not allow the Clarks to move to the Naga village. For the next three years, Rev. Clark had to supervise from a distance the work of Godhula among the people. Finally, in March of 1876, Rev. Clark went up to Dekha Haimong village to settle there. Living among the people as a foreigner was not easy. He, too, was suspected of

Figure 7. Naga Men in Ordinary Costume. Photo by E. W. Clark, for *A Corner in India*. Reproduced with permission of the American Baptist Foreign Mission Society (The society is now known as International Ministries).

being a spy for the British government. There was also strong opposition to the Christian way of life, because the new believers were not willing to work on the Sabbath. They were not willing to take heads anymore or to make sacrifices to the spirits of the trees and to the spirits of the earth.

Mrs. Clark recorded Godhula's comments regarding the effects of sacrifices on the Nagas' health. Godhula had noticed that the people of the village were, in general, malnourished, despite the fact that they had gardens and animals. He observed that they were sacrificing their animals and their vegetables to the spirits so often that they were depriving themselves of good food, frequently having only one meal a day.[7]

After only eight months of living in the village, Rev. Clark and his small band of believers realized that they needed to leave Dekha Haimong and establish a new village. They were experiencing persecution and resentment from some of the villagers, which was causing division and unrest throughout the village. They decided to strike out on their own to find a new place to live. The little congregation left the confines of the village on October 24, 1876, and prayed for protection through the night in the jungle. The next day, after some hours of difficult climbing, they arrived at the crest of the mountain, where they determined to establish the village of Molung.

Narola showed us a document related to the establishment of the new village. She explained that Rev. Clark had written up a list of rules, to which the leaders of the group agreed to adhere in the new village of Molung. Based on their experience of living in Dekha Haimong, it was evident to Rev. Clark and others that superstitions and certain practices of the past needed to be renounced by the people. Also, they needed to agree on things like taxes and land ownership. Unbelievers were allowed to live in the new village, but they had to agree to live by the rules: no skulls, no pagan burials, no rice beer, no sacrifices to the spirits.[8]

In the new village, each family could choose their own place to build a house and have a small garden. Much of the land, however, was reserved for future residents, whom they hoped would join them from their old village. The Clarks' home was made of bamboo and thatch, just like the other homes in the village, except that it was larger.

Edward Clark had already begun the work of transcribing the spoken language of the Nagas into a phonetic written language. He continued this work the entire time he lived in Nagaland. A reading primer was the first book to be printed in 1877, followed by a catechism. The printing press

Figure 8. The Clarks' Mission Bungalow in Molung. Photo by E.W. Clark for book, *A Corner in India*. Reproduced with permission of the American Baptist Foreign Mission Society.

was brought up the mountain to Molung in 1883, and the Gospels of Matthew and John and a Naga hymnbook were printed soon thereafter.

Narola's great grandfather, Ao Kilep, became the first Naga pastor. He helped Rev. Clark with language translation and with the compilation of an Ao-Naga Dictionary. This was an impressive, major work, which was published in 1911. Rev. Edward W. Clark received a Doctor of Divinity degree, D.D., from Brown University 1901. He received honorary doctorates from two other universities, as well.

Mary Mead Clark, Educator

Mary Mead Clark is credited with teaching the Naga people to read. Narola shared with us that in order to motivate her pupils to come to school, Mrs. Clark would invite them to her house where they helped her cut out cookies in the shape of an A. Then she would let them eat the baked cookies and would say, "Come back tomorrow and we will learn to make the next letter, B." She certainly was creative in motivating them to learn to read.[9]

Mary Mead Clark is considered to be the Founder of Education in Nagaland, because she started the first school in 1878. Today her picture hangs in the Nagaland Department of Education. An elementary school has been named in her honor and a monument has been erected to give her recognition for her efforts in the education of the Naga people. Mary Mead Clark is also credited for "opening the mouths of the Naga women."

The early converts were men, but the Clarks knew that women should hear the gospel message, too, and that they should be educated, as well. The first Naga women to publicly confess their Christian faith were in Mrs. Clark's school for young women.[10]

Narola told us that, on the Annual Missions Day, which is October 24, the people of the village of Molung, now called Molungyimsen, honor the Clarks with a morning church service, singing hymns and praying for how they can more effectively reach others with the gospel. In the afternoon, they have a service of celebration for the "opening of the mouths of the Naga women," their way of saying Women's Liberation. Mary Mead Clark herself was ahead of her time, in that she insisted on including her first and maiden name in her name, rather than be known only as Mrs. Edward Clark.[11]

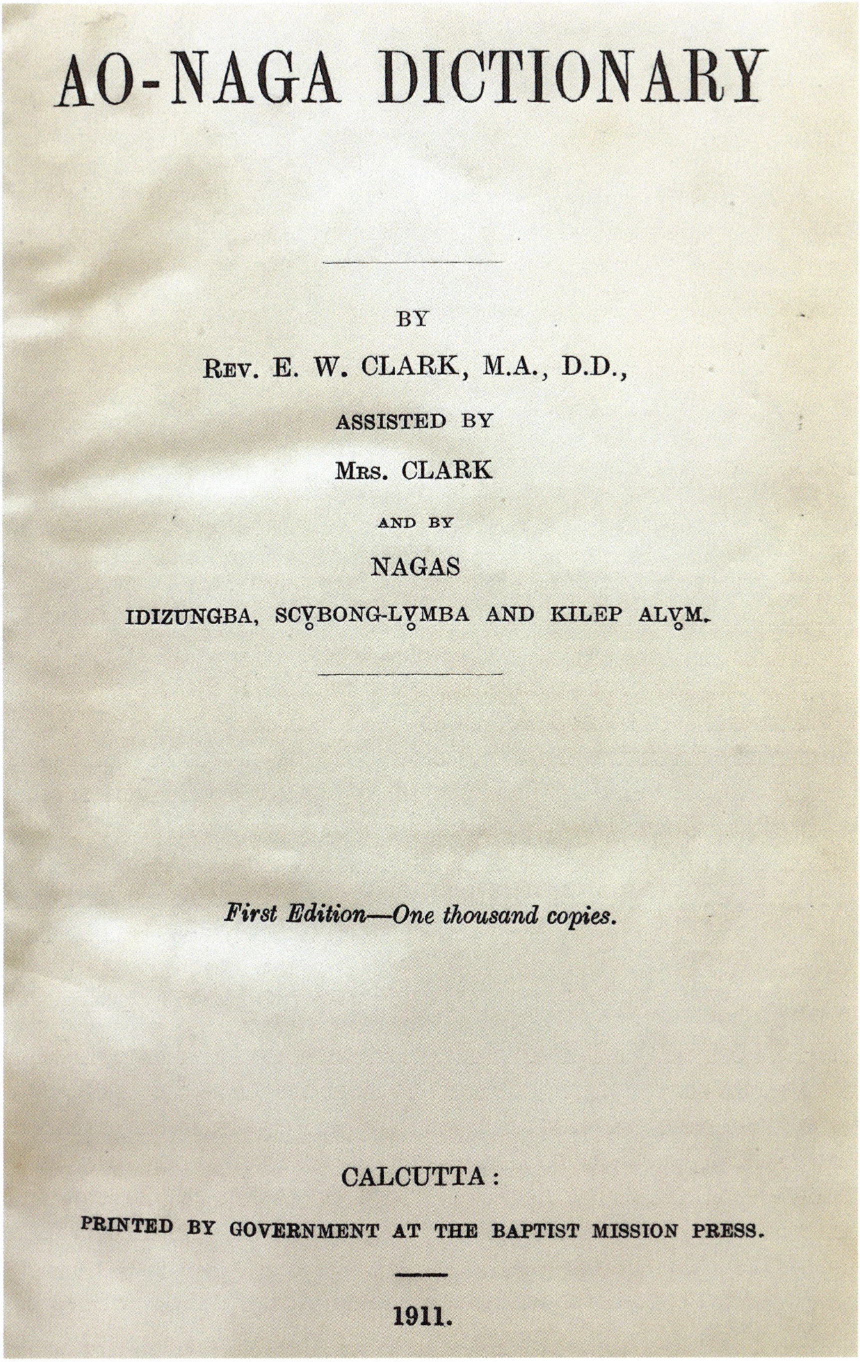

AO-NAGA DICTIONARY

BY

Rev. E. W. CLARK, M.A., D.D.,

ASSISTED BY

Mrs. CLARK

AND BY

NAGAS

IDIZUNGBA, SCU̱BONG-LU̱MBA AND KILEP ALU̱M.

First Edition—One thousand copies.

CALCUTTA:
PRINTED BY GOVERNMENT AT THE BAPTIST MISSION PRESS.

1911.

Figure 9. The title page of Rev. Clark's *Ao Naga Dictionary* with the names of the translation assistants, including Narola Ao McFayden's ancestor, Ao Kilep. Photo by E.C. Strauss

Rev. Clark's Impact on Agriculture and Rural Development

Rev. Clark was innovative in the areas of agriculture and rural development. Among other things, he encouraged the people to plant fruit trees. A lychee tree, which was planted in the Clark's courtyard in 1878, is still producing fruit in abundance today, so much so that the church at Molungyimsen sends baskets of fruit to neighboring congregations, with the challenge to be fruitful for God, just as the Clarks' tree is fruitful, year after year.

Figure 10. Clark Suspension Bridge. Photo by Imkongakum, 2018. Collection of Narola Ao McFayden and Kenneth McFayden,

With the help of the Naga men and with materials shipped from America, Rev. Clark built a steel cable suspension bridge over the Milak River, in 1888. The story is told that after the Naga men had carried the heavy cable up the mountain, they sat down and cried, despairing over such a crazy idea as constructing a bridge out of cable. They had to see it to believe it. The bridge is still in use today. Instead of being cut off from all travel during the rainy season, as was the case before the bridge was built, the Naga people are able to travel and have commerce in other villages all year round.[12]

Figure 11. Clark Theological College in Mokokchung. Photo by Imkongakum, 2018. Collection of Narola Ao McFayden and Kenneth McFayden.

Rev. Edward Clark established the first secondary school in the village of Impur. He also founded the Clark Theological College in Mokokchung, a town more centrally located and accessible to students coming from other areas to attend Bible college. Narola attended this college before coming to the United States for graduate school. By a remarkable coincidence, I recently met a young woman from Bhutan, who was here in Dutchess County at the behest of the Queen of Bhutan. She had attended the Clark College in Nagaland as well.

The Village of Molungyimsen Today

The village of Molungyimsen, has recently been designated as the Heritage Village of Nagaland. School children and youth groups visit the town to learn of their heritage. They visit the Clark Museum to see the printing press wheel and some of the Clarks' personal items, like Mrs. Clark's cast iron bathtub. The students also visit the site of the Clarks' house, which today is marked by the Clark Light Tower and the Clark's Lychee Tree. The small congregation, which began in 1876, has grown and endured through the generations. A beautiful, modern church was built in Molungyimsen in 2013.[13]

When Narola was invited by the North East and Amenia Historical Societies to present the Naga story in April 2015, she shared a few current statistics. She reported that about 90% of the people in Nagaland are Christians. There are over 15,000 Baptist churches with almost 520,000 baptized members. Nagaland is the only Christian province in India. The other provinces are predominantly Buddhist, Hindu, Muslim, or animist.[14]

In recent decades, the Naga churches have sent missionaries to neighboring countries and to other parts of India. Naga students have come to America for post-graduate education. I know of at least one Naga pastor now ministering in New Hampshire. This past summer 2018, a missionary couple working with the Hmong people in Thailand, contacted me for a "pilgrimage tour" of Amenia and North East. Both were Naga citizens and graduates of the Clark College.

Figure12. Ao Naga Young People Visit the Heritage Village of Molungyimsen. Photo by Imkongakum, 2018. Collection of Narola Ao McFayden and Kenneth McFayden.

The Amenia Historical Society Presentation in 2015

Attending Narola's historical society presentation in 2015 were two near relatives of the Clarks. One relative was a grand-nephew of Dr. Clark, Jon Barrett, who lives in North East and has in his possession an authentic Naga spear, that was given to his father by the Clarks. The second

Figure 13. Narola Ao and Ken McFayden in Amenia, 2015. Photo by J. Rossman, North East Historical Society, North East, NY.

relative was a grand-niece of Mrs. Mary Mead Clark, Helen Benham Kim. Helen was raised in Amenia, but now lives in New Jersey. In 2018, this descendant of the Mead family, gave to Amenia Historical Society an impressive collection of original books in the Ao-Naga language, which were compiled and printed by Dr. and Mrs. Clark, as well as photos, letters and memorabilia of the Clarks.

Although visiting the graves of the Clarks was of utmost importance to her, Narola told us that she was sent by the Naga people to personally thank the Towns of North East and Amenia for sending Edward and Mary Mead Clark to the Naga Hills over a century ago. She came to tell us of the transformative work of the Clarks in her country, which is still evident today. As a seminary professor, Narola Ao McFayden, Ph.D., is herself an example of that work.

[1] Joel Benton, Editor, Amenia Seminary Reunion (New York: Broadway Publishing Co., 1907), pp. 17-24, 44, 62.

[2] Benton, pp. 85-88.

[3] Mary Mead Clark, A Corner in India (Philadelphia: American Baptist Publication Society, 1907), pp. 5-7.

[4] Mary Mead Clark, pp. 7-8.

[5] Mary Mead Clark, pp. 9-10, 46-48.

[6] Mary Mead Clark, pp. 10-12.

[7] Mary Mead Clark, pp. 11-12, 140-141.

[8] Narola Ao McFayden, Oral Presentation to Amenia and North East Historical Societies, April 12, 2015.

[9] NarolaAo McFayden, Oral Presentation.

[10] Narola Ao McFayden, Ph.D., Traveling in Time with Pioneers of Our Faith Edward Winter Clark and Mary Mead Clark (North Charleston, SC: CreateSpace Independent Publishing Platform, 2016), pp. 44-47.

[11] NarolaAo McFayden, Oral Presentation.

[12] Mary Mead Clark, pp. 128-130.

[13] Narola Ao McFayden, Oral Presentation.

[14] Narola Ao McFayden, Oral Presentation.

DCHS Yearbooks Open Windows into "Invisible" Black Community

by Bill Jeffway

When Lorraine M. Roberts and Lawrence H. Mamiya wrote a history of Poughkeepsie's Black community for the Dutchess County Historical Society (DCHS) Yearbook in 1987, they headlined it "Invisible People, Untold Stories." Their point was that many of the stories of the Black community are not written into our history books or held in our community consciousness. That goes to the heart of our DCHS' philosophy that only a genuine and whole understanding of the past can best inform the present and prepare us for the future.

Figure 1. An undated image of the children's choir at AME Zion Church. N.d. Photograph. Collection of the Dutchess County Historical Society, Walter Patrice Collection. Organized in 1837, the Church would become an important center for the African-American community. In 1910, the local businessmen, the Smith Brothers, of cough drop notoriety, gave the money for a new church to be built. It stands today as a Nationally Registered Landmark. The Church is known now as the Smith Metropolitan AME Zion Church.

DCHS Yearbooks for 1915 to 1989 Online

In what is arguably a small step in a much larger ambition to make these individuals and their stories more accessible, DCHS has completed the work of putting its yearbooks (the longest-running historical journal in New York State) fully available online for the years 1915 to 1989. You'll find a list of relevant articles called out elsewhere in this article. They can be found, with related items from the DCHS Collections and statistical information, at www.dchsny.org/slavery.

Another opportunity to "decode" the stories of our shared past is through the DCHS Walter Patrice Collection. Focusing on the history of a church that Mr. Patrice's family was involved in across three centuries—the AME Zion Baptist Church—this history can be viewed online at www.dchsny.org/AMEZion. Yet another way is to look at the African-American experience during and just after WWI at www.dchsny.org/WWI-african-american-exp. What you will discover among the stories and collections mentioned is that the earliest stories of the Black community are, of course, the stories of the enslaved. New York State, concerned with both the economic impact and social change involved in the abolition of slavery in the state, the passing of the "Gradual Abolition Act" of 1799, prevented full freedom until July 4, 1827. As a result, a large part of the story of the African-American community is one of its continuous quest for the promise of freedom and equality—a search too often blocked by powers beyond their control.

Among the DCHS Collections are "bills of sale." Persons, mothers, fathers, sons and daughters are listed in wills and estate inventory among other "property." It is, to say the least, difficult to imagine this as an accepted common practice. The enslaved in Dutchess County might have lived under the same roof as their owners, or, sometimes, in separate quarters. The birth of a slave mother's child might have been recorded in the slave-owner's family Bible. But there the proximity ends. Harsh, barbaric legal (and extra-legal) practices kept delineations painfully clear. No matter the quality of a slave's treatment, the salient point remained: he had no control over his own fate. He had to obey another human being constantly and without question to earn his daily bread.

The Expansion, Contraction, and Abolition of Slavery in Dutchess County

The Dutch were the first to bring African slaves to what they called New Amsterdam and New Netherland in the 1600s. And while there was a dedicated slave census in 1755, accurate numbers can be hard to pin down until the start of the every-ten-year U.S. Federal Census. Like the broader story of the economic growth of the county, the expansion of slavery developed first in the river towns, and then grew inland.

Something particular to Dutchess County is the dynamic of the countervailing pressure from Quaker-dominant towns such as Dover, Pawling, and Millbrook that prohibited slave-owning among members. A meeting in 1767 held at Quaker Hill (Pawling) started a process that gained strength in the early 1770s to prohibit "Friends" from being slave owners. Northern Dutchess felt the influx of Quakers, bringing the same principles to bear in the 1790s. The expansion of military facilities in southern Dutchess during the Revolutionary War prompted a move north to locations in Milan and Pine Plains.

So not surprisingly, in 1820, the last Federal Census before the New York State abolition of slavery, the town with the lowest number of slaves was the town of Dover, citing one slave in its census, out of the 67 persons of color. Pawling shows four slaves, out of 77 total persons of color. The other extreme, Fishkill, which included Beacon at the time, shows 266 slaves out of 691 persons of color. Red Hook shows 182 slaves among 300 persons of color.

The Revolutionary War was disruptive to the old aristocratic landlord/tenant farmer "problem" that had prevented much local land ownership. But it was not as immediately disruptive to the practice of slavery. During the period 1790 to 1820, the first Federal Census of the U.S., and the last before slavery was abolished in New York State in 1827, the numbers show a relatively stable population of persons of color, around 2,150 at the start of that period, and around 2,400 in the following decades. The change is the degree to which those persons of color were enslaved. In 1790, 82% of these persons were enslaved. Between 1800 and 1820 there was a gradual diminution: 1800: 63%; 1810: 52%; 1820: 31%. 1830: theoretically 0%.

A Case Study: Andrew Frazier of Pine Plains

With some exceptions, the conclusion of the Civil War saw a shift of rural African Americans to cities where they found some strength in numbers and in association. The larger story is too big and complex to narrate here. But in summary, since one of the great powers of local history is its ability to bring a very personal experience and lens to major national trends, it is worth mentioning—perhaps one of our county's most extraordinary families, that of Revolutionary War veteran Andrew Frazier, whose descendants remain in the county today. He is referred to as "the colored man" in writing in the 1830s by no less than John Armstrong, the U.S. Secretary of War under President Madison, and U.S. Senator, among writings related to a friend's pension application.

Most likely born a slave, Andrew Frazier settled with the Graham family in what is now Pine Plains just prior to the Revolutionary War. Among his descendants who bore the Frazier family name and served the cause of freedom were four descendants who served in the Civil War (one died in service). Two great-great grandsons named Frazier served in WWI, and a great-great granddaughter founded the Women's Auxiliary to the Harlem Hellfighters in WWI. And a 6th generation veteran fought in WWII. Enlisting in 1943 he served in a segregated military unit, one which would not be integrated until 1948.

Articles published in DCHS Yearbooks relating to the African American experience in the county, free and enslaved.

"The Unknown Soldier—and the Unknown Hamilton Fish," by Sarah Gates, Vol. 97, 2018.

"Executive Order 9981," by David L. Goodwin, Volume 97, 2018.

"The Second Annual N.A.A.C.P. Meeting, Amenia, N.Y., by Julia Hotton, Volume 96, 2017.

"The Case and Times of Dred Scott," by John Barry, Volume 95, 2016.

"Dutchess County, New York and Beaufort County, North Carolina during the Civil War," by Peter S. Bedrossian, Volume 95, 2016.

"John A. Bolding, Fugitive Slave & John A. Bolding: The Rest of His Story," by Helen Wilkinson Reynolds (reprint) and Eileen Mylod Hayden, Volume 94, 2015.

"How Poughkeepsie Contributed to the Enlistment of Blacks in the Union Army," by Julia Hotton, Volume 93, 2014.

"Samuel Morse's Philosophy of Christian Slavery & A Poughkeepsie Lawyer Challenges Samuel Morse on Slavery," by Roger Donway, Vol.90, 2011.

"Wise Voices, Plain Speaking: Twentieth Century Griots," by Lorraine M. Roberts & Elieen M. Hayden, Volume 89, 2010.

"The Fugitive Slave Law of 1850," by Arun Banjeree, Volume 79, 1994.

"Invisible People, Untold Stories: Historical Overview of the Black Community in Poughkeepsie," by Lawrence H. Mamiya and Lorraine M. Roberts, Vol. 72, 1987.

"Slaveholding on Livingston Manor and Clermont," 1686-1800, by Roberta Singer, Vol. 69, 1984.

"The Fading Veneer of Equality: The Afro-American Experience in Poughkeepsie Between 1840 and 1860," Vol. 68, 1983.

"The Civil War Comes to Dutchess County," by David Lund, Vol. 67, 1982.

"Separate Black Education in Dutchess County," by Carlton Mabee, Vol. 65, 1980.

"Ante-Bellum Dutchess County's Struggle Against Slavery," by Susan J. Crane, Vol. 65, 1980.

"The Old Plantation," by Burton Coon, originally published July 4, 1925, Volume 64, 1979.

"Uncle Tom," by Burton Coon, originally published April 4, 1925, Volume 64, 1979.

"Dutchess County Quakers and Slavery," *1750-1830*, by Dell Upton. Vol. 55, 1970.

"The Public Career of James Talmadge," Vol. 45, 1960.

"The Anti-Slavery Movement in Dutchess County, 1835-1850," by Amy Pearce Ver Nooy, 1943.

"The Negro in Dutchess County in the Eighteenth Century," by Helen Wilkinson Reynolds, Vol. 26, 1941.

"John Bolding a Fugitive Slave," by Helen Wilkinson Reynolds, Vol. 20, 1935.

Brief, but illuminating references to the enslaved and African American experience in the county.

Remarks of Isaac S. Wheaton at Lithgow, 1922, (slave – p. 23).

Amenia One Hundred Years Ago. 1922, (slave – p. 31).

Old Brown Homestead in "The Orchard," 1924, (Joe Legg, slave – p. 55).

The Growth of Dutchess County in the Eighteenth Century, 1926, (racial population statistics, pp 27-29).

Captain Israel Smith, 1926, (will names enslaved, p. 46).

Madam Brett's Discarded Will, 1927, (ref. enslaved, p. 33).

Colonel James Van Der Burgh, 1930, (enslaved, pp. 41-43).

A Dutchess County Gardener's Diary, 1829-1866, 1936, (pp. 63-66).

Francis Filkin's Book: A Key to Part of Its Contents, 1938, ref. enslaved p. 54, pp. 59-60).

Slaves (a list of slaves in the Hyde Park Patent), 1939, pp. 87-88.

The Town of Clinton, 1941, (slaves, pp. 50-52).

An Account of the Eastern and Southeastern Portions of the Town of Hyde Park, 1942, (persons of color, p. 30).

The General Store at Salt Point, 1848-1849, 1944, (George Hams, "colord man" – p. 43).

The Federal Census – A Research Inventory, 1981, (slaves in Clinton, Hyde Park, Pleasant Valley, pp. 126-139).

The 1714 Dutchess County Census: Measure of Household Size, 1983, (slaves, pp. 173-174).

Alfred Ackert and the Dutchess County Society of New York, 1984, (slavery abolished, p. 123).

Robert Newlin Verplanck: Civil War Hero in Changing Times, 2012, (education, pp. 120-123; black soldiers, p. 123).

Raise High the Roof Beam, Carpenter: Profile of a Consummate Volunteer

Interview by John Desmond

Richard Taylor is a happy man when he is standing on a building site. Rich is an excellent carpenter and loves watching a building going up. I visited him as he watched—no scrutinized—volunteers install roof trusses and plywood for a new pavilion located at the southern trail head of the Dutchess County Rail Trail in Hopewell Junction. The finished pavilion will provide a place for runners, walkers, and cyclists on the Rail Trail to sit, rest, eat, and drink in the shade out of the weather. Rich told me that, "Normally, I would be up there straddling the roof beam but, at eighty and with a bum foot, I'm down here on the ground taking photographs." Rich is an especially happy man when he volunteers: whether to renovate a house, redesign a railroad bridge into a walkway, restore a railroad depot, or as in this case raise a pavilion. He is a consummate volunteer improving properties in Dutchess County—and around the United States—one by one.

Figure 1. The Bernard Rudberg Pavilion under Construction, Hopewell Junction, New York, 2018. Photo by John Desmond.

John Desmond: Before Rich chronicled his several volunteer projects and experiences, he wanted to report on his childhood and young manhood in Dutchess County. Where he lived and how he lived, he told me, has motivated his volunteer efforts all his adult life.

Childhood in Millbrook, New York

Rich Taylor: I was born as a twin in 1938 at Vassar Hospital. My twin's name was Robert. We grew up with our older brother, Charles, and our parents, Mary Rogers and Charles Taylor, living in a barn with red board and batten siding and with hand-split, heavy shakes, yet without electricity, central heat, and running water, on Shady Dell Road in Millbrook, New York. Our bedroom was on the third floor next to the hay loft, and as kids, we would hide in there at times. In the winter, it was as cold in the bedroom as it was outside. My mother would tuck us in every night with heated bricks, wrapped in towels, and with two heavy quilts over my twin brother and me to keep us warm. The bricks were heated on the wood-burning stove in the front room downstairs on the second floor, the only source of heat in the un-insulated barn-house. Cooking was on a kerosene stove, and lighting was supplied by kerosene lamps. For our weekly bath, mother had to heat hot water on the kerosene stove and carry it up the winding staircase to the bathroom. Our family had one cow for milk, one pig, and many chickens.

Figure 2. The Barn-house where the Taylor family lived, only slightly changed from the 1940s. Photo by John Desmond, 2018. Taylor Family Collection.

When Robert and I were born, my family was on Dutchess County assistance. I don't know all the financial details, but I think we were living there in the barn free with the help of George Whalen, a Millbrook bank owner, who also owned the barn, and with the help from the Federated Church of Millbrook. Growing up as twins, Robert and I did everything together: playing around the barn; hiking in the woods; running along the stream at the old Millbrook Mill located on the corner of Shady Dell Road and Route 44; and watching the horses in the basement stalls, which was actually the first-floor of the barn. We were happy. Robert and I slept in the same bed; Charles, our older brother, slept in another bed in the same room. As I mentioned, we did have a bathroom upstairs with water by hand pump.

Figure 3. Rich (left) and Rob (right) Taylor as three-year olds. Photo taken outside the barn-house, 1941. Taylor Family Collection.

In 1944, at age six, Robert and I walked almost a mile to a one-room school house, the Shady Dell School, where we attended first and second grades. At the school, about thirty students of different ages were taught by one teacher who lived nearby. Charles Simonsen, a classmate of my brother and me, reminded me that the pupils brought their own soup from home and at lunchtime, heated their soup on the stove. The school still stands there. At one time, I wanted to restore it as a museum because of its unique construction and because I attended school there. However, George Whalen, the same man who owned the barn-house in which we lived, did not want to part with it, let alone let me restore it. He wanted to use it as housing for his hired help. It has since been sold. Two years ago, in 2016, I stopped there and had a nice visit with the owner. This man, a teacher, took me on a tour inside the school house, pointing out to me that the main classroom was kept intact. I was glad that the main classroom had not been destroyed. I saw the spot where my desk was located—I think. My visit to the schoolhouse brought back fond memories.

My mother was of average height, thin, with blonde hair, and wore glasses. She had to go to work, so we could get off Dutchess County assistance. First, she got a job at Schatz Federal Bearing Company in Poughkeepsie, inspecting ball bearings. We had no car, so mother walked over a mile to the intersection of Shady Dell Road and Route 44 to get a ride from a co-worker to her job at Schatz. Then she got the job as a cook on the Wheaton estate and farm in Lithgow, New York, a hamlet in Dutchess County, approximately four miles west of Amenia. As part of her compensation, she was given a house. So in 1945, when Robert and I were seven, our family moved from the barn-house into a real house. The house in Lithgow was a story and a half with three bedrooms upstairs, stucco siding, and a large ice house out back. We did have electric light and all. We did not have a refrigerator but had an ice box. It was my brother's and my job to keep the ice box full with ice from the ice house.

Figure 4. Shady Dale Road One-Room School House where the Taylor boys attended school in the 1940s. Photo by John Desmond, 2018. Taylor Family Collection.

My father was of average height and heavy from lack of outdoor activity and from heavy smoking. He had suffered a serious back injury in a well-drilling accident in Millbrook, New York and could not work for twenty-one years. He could walk with a cane, did the housework and cooking for the family, but could not get a job. My father always had a garden when we lived both on Shady Dale Road and in Lithgow. He used the hoe as a cane and hooked his cane in his belt. He had a large garden the size of an acre. My brother and I worked in the garden weeding and cultivating using our Bolens Garden two- wheel garden tractor. We grew all our food except for meat and staples. We had a large freezer where my mother stored her frozen food from the garden. She also canned some foods. My twin brother and I raised chickens and sold them as fryers in the fall to our neighbors. We were featured in the Bolen's Magazine with a write-up and pictures of our gardening, canning, and such.

My father had a limited education. He was born, grew up, and met my mother on Nantucket Island. I do not know why they moved from Nantucket to Dutchess County. In 1948, my father was hired by IBM as a parts inspector, his first job in twenty-one years after the accident. At the time, IBM was one of the few businesses hiring disabled people. With both parents employed, we now were able to purchase a car, a 1939 Nash, which we bought from Herb Redl who had a garage in Arlington. My mother would drive my father to and from work every day as well as drive herself to her job as a cook on the estate where we lived. She did all the driving since my father could not drive after his accident. By the following year, 1949, my parents had worked their way off Dutchess County assistance and were able to buy some land with an unfinished house sitting on it in La Grangeville, New York. That house was a block basement; with a flat, tar-paper roof; but no insulation. It was heated with a hot-air furnace.

Young Adulthood

In 1957, when I was eighteen, I became the only one in my family to graduate from Arlington High School. I did so with honors, ranking in the upper-third of my class. During my senior year I worked at IBM in their co-op program for half a day and earned $1.50 an hour. I joined the Army in my senior year of high school for six months of active duty and then six years of Army Reserve. I took basic training at Fort Dix and then went to Fort Knox for armor training (tanks). After my six months of active duty, I returned home yet still lived in sub-standard conditions at the La Grangeville house until I was twenty-two. I found a job at Grand Union as a cashier-checker. I could not stand the monotony of constantly checking the prices of grocery items and cashing out the customers. Three months of that, and I searched for another job.

The Taylor Story

We grow our own food on Miracle Acre

by Bert Burns

The "Mighty Mite", the Bolens Power-Ho became as much a member of the Taylor family as Pudgy the dog, and Mickey, the cat.

It's only an acre of land, no more fertile than the thousands of acres that surround it just outside the city of Poughkeepsie, N. Y., but to Mr. and Mrs. Charles W. Taylor and their three boys, it's truly a "Miracle Acre."

In the three years that the Taylor family has worked that small area, it has brought not only a saving of more than $1,500 in food bills, but has resulted in the steady recuperation of Mr. Taylor from a malady which doctors long since had said was "too far gone."

"Miracle Acre" had its birth about two and a half years ago after the Taylors had moved to their present home from Millbrook, N. Y. Mr. Taylor, although partially crippled with arthritis, had obtained a job as inspector at the International Business Machines Corporation plant in Poughkeepsie and the move was designed to bring him closer to his place of work. But the venture was a gamble. For eighteen years previous, Mr. Taylor hadn't been able to work. His wife had held various positions as a cook, making just enough to provide the minimum of food and clothing for the family.

One night, Mr. Taylor gathered his little family around him. There was Charles, now 22, and the twins, Robert and Richard, now 14, and his wife.

"This is a decision we all have to make," he said. "We have no money. To get this land, we'll have to work and work and work. But, in the end, we'll have something that's ours and Ours alone."

The decision was unanimous.

The Taylors bought eight acres on their present site, contracted for building their present one-story home and racked their brains for means of not only beating the high cost of living, but of saving money as well. Finally, they hit on the idea of their garden. If successful, it at least would mean a saving on the food bill.

The slow, laborious work began. Since Mr. Taylor worked his full eight hours a day and the boys went to school, all the farm work had to be done at night or on Saturday. And the land was stoney and covered with brush. Something had to be done.

It was Mrs. Taylor who accidently ran across the solution. While shopping in Poughkeepsie one Saturday, she walked into a demonstration of the Bolens Power-Ho Tractor. After seeing what it did during the demonstration and after talking to the demonstrator she knew it, and it alone, was the one thing which would speed the success of their garden and directly of their new venture.

It took another family conclave, but the result was the same. The "mighty mite", the Bolens Power-Ho, became as much a member of the Taylor family as Pudgy, the dog, and Micky, the cat.

With the tractor, the family cleared off their "Miracle Acre", hauling off the stones, cutting down the tall grass, doing the light plowing, and effecting the cultivation. It went smoothly and, what was more important, fast, thanks to the new member of the family, the "mighty mite."

In one season, all the work and planning paid off. The yield produced more than 1,000 pounds of frozen vegetables, enough to supply the family from one year to the next. Mrs. Taylor packed her home freezer and was

Figure 5. "The Taylor Story." Bolens' Article with Photo of Taylor Family and Bolen Two-wheel Garden Tractor. 1952. Advertisement in Spring Issue, 1953, *Suburban Squire*. Bolens Division. Taylor Family Collection.

Figure 6. La Grangeville House occupied by the Taylor family, Painting, c. 1950. Taylor Family Collection.

In the spring of 1958, I was hired by Eberhard Builders. I started as a laborer and within six months was promoted to construction foreman and given a crew of five men all older than myself. Despite the differences in our ages, the older men and I got along well, and we built many houses. I worked for Eberhard for eleven years until 1969, and then I decided to start my own construction business, Shelter Update Construction, which I have owned and operated for forty-nine years. In 1960, while working for Eberhard, I married my wife, Maureen, and moved to an apartment in Poughkeepsie after living in sub-standing housing for twenty-two years. We both disliked living in the third-floor apartment, since we both grew up in the country. Thus, we built our first house in 1962 in Wappingers Falls. We had two children, Rick, now fifty-six, and Lauri, now fifty-three. In 1963, I ended my time in the Army Reserve after six years of summer camps.

Both my brothers, Charles and Robert, had jobs also, and were married. My mother and father both worked into their sixties. My father died at the age of sixty-three, and my mother passed away at ninety-seven. Charles died in 2008, and Rob passed in 2015. After my father passed away, I used all my skills as a builder to construct a nice house on the old foundation of the unfinished La Grangeville house and moved my mother into this new house. Then, I refinished the old basement apartment into a fine one-bedroom apartment complete with every modern appliance. My mother moved back downstairs where she would have no stairs to climb to enter and exit the house.

Starting to Volunteer with Youth Groups

John Desmond: As your son and daughter, Rick and Lauri, grew up, they joined various youth groups along the way, isn't that so? And, as I remember, you, Rich, and your wife, Maureen, began volunteering with those same groups, typical of many parents the world over.

Rich Taylor: Yes. Rick joined Indian Guides in 1971. Along with Rick, I joined the Indian Guides, and we began doing organized projects together while also helping others. We all worked together making an Indian head dress decorated with feathers and beads. I still have it today.

Figure 7. The Indian Head Dress Rich Taylor and son Rick, working with the Indian Guides, created this headpiece. 1970s. Taylor Family Collection.

As Rick grew older, he joined first Cub Scouts then Boy Scouts. With both scouting groups, I volunteered. We camped; made small, wooden car racers; fashioned antique wooden tools; and picked up junk with my dump truck to sell and raise money for the troupe. The wooden plane, which we made out of a tree limb, we later sold to an antique dealer at the Stormville Flea Market. Years later, while attending a conference in Sheraton, Massachusetts I saw the plane in their collage of old items.

After my son graduated from college in 1985, we had time to start hiking and camping in the Catskills and Adirondacks. Eventually, we got interested in winter hiking and camping. In 1986, we joined the Adirondack Mountain Club Winter Mountaineering School. We took the course on winter hiking and camping, and, even later in 1987, volunteered to help others wanting to learn how to survive in cold climates.

Habitat for Humanity and President Jimmy Carter

Laurie was interested in dancing and singing but later became more interested in volunteering. She joined me on Habitat builds, working on both Jimmy Carter and local Habitat projects. We also went on birding trips near and far and Zip-Line rides.

Figure 8. Rich and son Rick winter camping, c. 1980s. Photo. Taylor Family Collection.

Figure 9. Rich and daughter Lauri on Habitat Builds in 1995. Photo. Taylor Family Collection.

I had grown up in the New Hackensack Reformed Church after moving to LaGrange in 1949 when I was eleven. Maureen and I attended services on a regular basis, especially as Rick and Lauri were growing up. So, in 1975, I joined the Building-and-Grounds Committee and shared my carpentry talents to help maintain the property on Route 376.

John Desmond: As with his job as a carpenter for Eberhard Builders, Rich rapidly learned what projects these various groups required of their participants, promptly assumed a leadership role within the groups, and gradually became an instructor for new participants. Perhaps you could tell us about your involvement with your major volunteer projects: the Habitat for Humanity, the Repairs Ministry, the Walkway over the Hudson, and the Hopewell Junction Railroad Depot.

Rich Taylor: In 1988, I read an article about Habitat for Humanity International's mission of eliminating sub-standard housing throughout the world. That mission was close to my heart because of my own experience with sub-standard living conditions for twenty-two years. I started supporting the organization with money donations. But when I heard that the state affiliate in New Hampshire was building a house in Warren and seeking volunteers, I joined up for the week-long build. That Habitat build was my first experience working with non-skilled volunteers for seven days during a Fourth of July week. At the first meeting, the president of the state affiliate said to all of us that, "if there are any professional builders here, please do not express your ways of building to the house leader." In other words, keep your mouth shut. So I said nothing about building houses, even though I had built hundreds.

I worked that first day with the President of the New Hampshire State Affiliate. We had a good time discussing how we would build the cellar stairs. Finally, he settled on my way. The house leader, who was a boat builder with no experience in building houses, was leading a large crew of non-skilled volunteers putting up the outside walls using inadequate bracing. He then had the volunteers load all of the roof trusses up-side-down on the walls. With poorly braced walls, the weight of the trusses blew the walls apart. So the volunteer workers had to remove the trusses and re-brace the walls. I had been watching from below and knew this was going to happen, but I stuck to my word not to say anything.

That evening at dinner, we all were asked where we were from and what kind of work we did. You can imagine the response from the President and the house leader after I told them I was a house builder. From then on, I became the second house leader, showing the way on tasks that the leader knew very little about. I had a great time teaching all the volunteers on how correctly to build a house. I had the best time of my life working with other volunteers who had the same feelings of helping to eliminate sub-standard housing as I did. This is when I contacted that wonderful disease "Infectious Habitius."

Since I caught this disease, I couldn't wait to do a Jimmy Carter Work Project. As soon as the Jimmy Carter Habitat for Humanity Work Projects announced in the Habitat newspaper that Jimmy was going to build ten houses in five days in Washington, D. C., I signed up to work as a crew leader. Being a crew leader let me work directly with other volunteers. The house leader had me install imitation brick with a woman who did cake decorating. When it came to putting the grout between the brick, she said I can do that because I'm a cake decorator. And she did a wonderful job! Another time I was installing roof shingles with two nuns from Maine. They wanted me to show them everything about house building. We had a good time and a lot of laughs.

I have several stories of working with Jimmy Carter himself. In Eagle Butte, South Dakota, we built thirty homes in five days for members of the Sioux Indian Nation living there in run-down, HUD housing. I was the house leader on house seventeen, and, of course, Jimmy was on house one. Jimmy came by my house after I had built my back steps and asked me if I had any treated lumber that I didn't need for him to build his back steps. I said, "Take a look in our scrap pile. I think there are a few pieces in there." My wife, Maureen, happened to be paying a visit at the time and offered to help him look for what he needed. That night at supper, Jimmy walked by, so I asked him how he made out with his steps. He replied, "I did one better than you, Rich. I put a railing on mine."

At this point, Rich's wife, Maureen joined the conversation:

Maureen Taylor: When Jimmy asked Rich if he had any treated lumber, I offered to help Jimmy look for the size of lumber he needed. Jimmy was very down to earth and thanked me for helping him. Of course, the Secret-Service guys had their eyes on me to make sure I did not hit him over the head with a board. Jimmy was very easy to talk to and had a great personality.

Rich Taylor: Another evening, we were working on finishing the sheet rock, so it would be ready for taping the next morning. Jimmy stopped by to see if we were on schedule. I said we should have the sheet rock mostly completed by 10:00 PM. He said I suggest you stay on it until it is all installed and ready for taping. I turned to the crew, who were all watching from doorways, and said you heard him; I guess we will be here to 11:00 or later. After the house was completed, one of the Sioux Chiefs walked through it carrying burning sweet grass to chase out evil spirits from all the corners.

At Eagle Butte, we stayed in two-person pup tents, over 500 of them, lined up on the high school's football field. Luckily, I had brought our Habitat Guide-on, a small, pointed flag on a pole, and had it by our tent to help us find the tent in the dark. By the way, Jimmy ate all his meals with us and slept in a large teepee near us. His Secret Service agents ate in restaurants and slept in motor homes near the teepee.

Figure 10. Maureen and Rich Taylor at Habitat for Humanity in Eagle Butte, SD, c. 1990. Photo. Taylor Family Collection.

I have witnessed two sexist men while building houses with Habitat. One worked on a Jimmy Carter Build in Alabama where I signed on as a general volunteer. Monday morning we all stood around the foundation listening to directions from the house leader. He told all the men to get up on the deck and start putting up the exterior walls. He told all the women

RAISE HIGH THE ROOF BEAM, CARPENTER 117

Figure 11. The teepee of Former President Jimmy Carter when working at Habitat for Humanity in Eagle Butte, SD. Taylor Family Collection.

Figure 12. Habitat for Humanity Blitz Build, Eagle Butte, SD, 1990. Photo. Taylor Family Collection. Former President Jimmy Carter in front row, center. Rich Taylor in second row, far right.

to stay on the ground and watch until the walls were all in place. I did not like what I was hearing, so I spoke up and asked him if the women could at least get up on the deck and do the toe nailing. His reply was NO! From then on, I could tell he did not like me and treated me with less respect. Most of the women did not like him and wanted to work with me after that.

I went to a Georgia build with a friend who later became my Vice President when we started our own Habitat for Humanity affiliate in Dutchess County, called Habitat for Humanity of Southern Dutchess. We started our affiliate in 1994. In the spring of 1995, I organized a sixty-mile, three-day walk to help raise awareness of the need to address the sub-standard living conditions of some children in Dutchess County and to raise awareness of a solution to that problem. That was the reason I organized Habitat for Humanity of Southern Dutchess. We built our first house in early summer 1995 as a seven-day Blitz Build with eighty volunteers. In 1997, we merged with the Poughkeepsie Habitat group and changed our name to Habitat for Humanity of Dutchess County.

During the blitz-building, I found time to organize the Repairs Ministry for helping the elderly with safety and weatherization issues. I learned they were living in poor conditions and did not have enough money to pay a contractor to do the needed repairs. I started doing repairs on two houses for two elderly women. These were one-day repair projects held on a Saturday and, with the correct number of volunteers, were completed in one day. The elderly homeowners paid for the materials and provided some sweat equity, but the labor was free. We were doing one project a month in the beginning. Other volunteer projects I organized include two trips to Mississippi after Hurricane Katrina and many Make-A-Difference day projects.

Walkway-over-the-Hudson

Also in 1995, I joined the Walkway over the Hudson organization as a board member and volunteered to work not only on the railroad bridge but also under it. On the bridge, I installed 8x8 ties on the beams and removed old railings. Under the bridge, I cut brush under the west-end of the bridge in Highland. I sold T-shirts at flea markets and other venues. I stayed with the project for three years, until 1998, but could see that it was not picking up any speed; in fact, it was failing. I left. Fred Schaffer, another board member and a Dutchess County lawyer, had good contacts with the right people who had money and connections. Fred saved that project. Thank goodness!

Figure 13. Maureen Taylor on the Highland-Poughkeepsie Railroad Bridge, 1996. Photo. Taylor Family Collection.

Hopewell Junction Railroad Depot

I discovered the abandoned and dilapidated Hopewell Junction Railroad Depot and started to find an interested group to save the station and restore it. I first became interested in the Depot in September 1995 when I came over to Philip Ortiz's in Hopewell Junction to have some welding done on my truck. I saw this decrepit and decaying building from across Ortiz's yard that looked like it might be a train station. I instantly knew this building had to be saved and restored. The next day I came back and took pictures of the Depot. The area around the Depot was being used as storage with piles of large pipes and steel panels. The place where the Depot was located was unattractive with other rundown buildings, a short road leading to an abandoned railroad bed, and a junk yard across from the railroad bed. No wonder no one seemed interested in it. A long seventeen years later, with many emotional and financial ups and downs, in April 2012, we opened the Visitors Center to the public. Six months later, the museum sections were open.

Figure 14. Abandoned and Dilapidated Hopewell Junction Depot the day after Rich Taylor saw it in 1995. Hopewell Junction, New York. Photo. Taylor Family Collection.

Charlie McDonald entered the conversation:

John Desmond: One day, as Rich and others worked on restoring the Depot, a walker on the Dutchess County Rail Trail, Charlie McDonald, noticed them at work, asked who was in charge, and was told to talk to Rich.

Charlie McDonald: I came up to Rich and asked what I could do to help. Rich said what can you do? I said I can do anything. Rich looked at me as if I were bragging. Rich gave me a job, and I did it well. Rich gave me another job, and I did it above and beyond what Rich asked me to do. Then Rich and I began working together on many jobs both large and small, from roofing a building to fixing a jammed cabinet.

John Desmond: Rich told me Charlie and he like to tease each other: "Charlie is from New York City," Rich said, "and I am, as you know by now, a country boy, so we tease each other about where we are from and what we know." Charlie told me, "Rich sometimes is kidding when he teases, and sometimes he is not kidding. You can tell whether he is kidding or not by his eyes." Nonetheless, both Rich and Charlie obviously enjoy working with each other.

Rich firmly claims that the principal motivation behind his several successful volunteer projects is a power and influence higher than his considerable skill as a carpenter and his seemingly boundless generosity and appealing good nature.

Rich Taylor: Volunteering is the way for me to help as many other people on this earth as I can with my God-given talents. Without God, I am nothing. God moved me to become a carpenter, starting with learning how to use a coping saw in sixth grade I can tell you stories where God saved the day when things went wrong on many of my Habitat builds. God caused me to say to the Depot Board that we are going out in faith and not stopping until the Depot is fully restored, knowing they had less than $1,000 in the checking account. God made me say to eighty volunteers at our first Habitat build in Beacon, New York, when a woman asked me what is going to happen if it rains, it will not rain. I knew the forecast was for rain all day, but I also knew God.

Maureen Taylor: I am very proud of Rich's volunteering, from the Indian Guides to the Hopewell Junction Depot. He has spent so much time at the Depot Restoration Project I threatened to put a cot over there, so he could sleep there.

John Desmond: Sir Kenneth Clark, the art critic, historian, lecturer, and museum curator explains why human beings think it worthwhile to build:

> [Civilization] requires confidence—confidence in the society in which one lives, belief in its philosophy, belief in its laws, and confidence in one's own mental powers. The way in which the stones of the Pont du Gard are laid is not only a triumph of technical skill, but shows a vigorous belief in law and discipline. Vigour, energy, vitality: all the great civilizations—or civilizing epochs—have had a weight of energy behind them..

When I left the building site of the pavilion on the southern trail head of the Dutchess County Rail Trail, late in the afternoon of the day I visited Rich, there was Rich standing inside under the newly installed roof, measuring a length of wood to be cut to size and fit somewhere. All the other volunteers had left. "You're not leaving?" I asked. "Not yet," he answered and waved good bye. Rich Taylor, the volunteer builder, has the technical skill, the belief in law and discipline, and the energy Kenneth Clark mentioned. He is, to paraphrase Clark, CIVILIZED.

[1] The title of this article is one letter off from the title of a novella by J. D. Salinger: *Raise High the Roofbeam, Carpenters*. That title, in turn, comes from a fragment by the Greek poet Sappho: "Raise high the roof beam, carpenters. Like Ares comes the bridegroom, taller far than a tall man."

[3] The following essay is based upon interviews: with Richard Taylor, Personal Interviews, 1-18 Aug., 1-18, 2018; Maureen Taylor, Personal Interview, Sept., 23, 2018; and Charles McDonald, Personal Interview Aug. 25, 2018.

[3] The estate and farm were managed by Isaac Smith Wheaton, the son of Dutchess County Judge Charles Wheaton who first owned the property.

[4] This organization, sponsored by the YMCA, is similar in purpose to the Boy Scouts, staffed primarily by volunteers, inspired by Native American culture and activities, and intended to support positive relationships between fathers and their children.

[5] A Roman aqueduct located in Provence, France.

[6] Kenneth Clark (Sir), Civilization (New York: Harper and Row, Publishers, 1969).

Locusts and Lincoln

by Margaret Duff

As you will see from this essay, the Locust Box actually contains the remains of, not locusts, but 17-year cicadas as well as political notices from the year 1860. It was part of a generous gift of Margaret Duff in 2009. I have seen the reactions of a number of people when they have viewed the Locust Box. Most recoil in disgust at the sight of 150-year-old insects encased in glass, not your usual entertainment in the early twenty-first century. I would encourage the reader, however, to think back to the nineteenth century when collecting and categorizing insects and other fauna and flora was a rather common occupation of intellectually curious laymen and scholars alike. What then might have been the significance of Benjamin Hall pairing these special animals with the election campaigns of the fall of 1860? Why did he do that?—C. Lewis, editor

How did Abraham Lincoln come together with locusts in this little box? On March 17, 1861, Benjamin Joseph Hall writes in his farm journal, "Made the Locust Box." I wonder if his sons, Reuben, age 8, and Preston, age 5, were watching or even helping? Why did Benjamin do this?

Figure 1. Benjamin J. Hall (1825-1896). N.d. Photograph. Collection of the Dutchess County Historical Society, Hall Family Collection.

Figure 2. The two sons of Benjamin J. Hall, Reuben and Preston: the older one, Reuben died in 1862, not quite a year after Benjamin made the Locust Box. N.d., probably c. 1855-56. Daguerrotype. Collection of the Dutchess County Historical Society, the Hall Family Collection.

Abraham Lincoln was elected in the same year that the 17-year locusts appeared on Benjamin Hall's farm in Dutchess County. Benjamin was one of those people who have to be busy all the time. He made a good farmer because of this. If he wasn't plowing, sowing the crops, or reaping, he was mending his stone walls, preparing locust wood posts for fencing or cleaning out his spring. Never an idle moment! After he put his 14 hives of bees in his cellar for the winter; after he made sure all the crops were in and prepared for sale or storage, and the hogs butchered, what would he do during the idle time?

Benjamin's farm journal, spanning the years 1851 through 1896, reveals this wide variety of skills. He would have known how to carve wood and work with glass and tools. In that year, he noted that he made a small chest, fixed a kettle, made a kitchen door, mended the boys' boots, fixed a hen roost and made a pen to kill hogs.

Why Put Cicadas (17-Year Locusts) in a Box?

But why would he put insects in a box? Benjamin had gone to the State Normal School in Albany after his local schooling through eighth grade in Clinton Corners. His Normal School papers and many of his books were saved and many are now in the Hall Family Collection at the Dutchess County Historical Society. You can see from these how many subjects were covered and the artistic flare he showed in his drawings. He left sketches of his own home and local buildings also.

He must have thought about this project for sometime. Probably the locusts in their larval and adult stages were collected in the fall of 1860; perhaps some were found clinging to the branches or on leaves after a hard fall freeze. A little research of the 17-year cicada shows that the larvae emerge from the ground where they have fed on roots of shrubs or trees for 16 years. They do this in the late spring—April through June—when the soil eight inches down has reached a temperature of about 64 degrees Fahrenheit. The insects climb trees to molt while shedding their larval "skin." In the tree they begin their chirping mating call. Eggs laid in twigs of the tree take about 10 weeks to hatch. Around August or September the larvae then crawl, or shower down from the trees and crawl into the ground for their 16-year maturation. These insects, though called locusts by the early European settlers in America, were actually cicadas, Family Cicadidae. The periodical cicadas were known as Magicidada. They might have seemed magical to the boys!

Since Benjamin made this box in mid March of 1861, it's almost certain that these insects preserved were from 1860. The 1860 or Brood II (of 12 Broods) will appear again in that area in 2030. 160 years from 1860 to

Figure 3. The Locust Box by Benjamin Hall. March, 1861. Wood, glass, insect carcasses, and newspaper advertisements for political races in 1860. Collection of the Dutchess County Historical Society, the Hall Family Collection. Photograph by Bill Jeffway.

2013 is 10 generations of 17-year locusts. Where I live in western Pennsylvania, Brood VIII is due to appear this spring (2019).

Perhaps the boys brought in the locusts on leaves and twigs in late summer and they were kept, as parents keep the "prizes" their children bring home. After Normal School, Benjamin had spent a year teaching in a one-room schoolhouse at school district #5 of the town of Washington. He was boarding with the Underhill family in Hibernia before being sent home in January 1851 with pneumonia. He never returned to teaching, but there can be little doubt that he would have been teaching his children as they worked around the farm.

Figure 4. The Locust Box by Benjamin Hall (close-up view showing ad for Abraham Lincoln for President and Hannibal Hamlin for Vice-President). March, 1861. Wood, glass, insect carcasses, and newspaper advertisements for political races in 1860. Collection of the Dutchess County Historical Society, the Hall Family Collection. Photograph by Bill Jeffway.

His journal is peppered with comments on the weather, seasonal anomalies, and observations about new inventions. He writes, "Went with Preston to see the steam shovel work." It would have been natural for him to tell his boys about the locusts and their strange habit of living underground for 16 years and coming out the 17th year. Since the 17-year Locust is the only variety that causes agricultural damage, as a farmer, he would have been especially aware of this phenomenon. He was 36 years old at this time and would have seen the locusts or heard of them once already. This would have been the first time for his sons.

There are some of Benjamin's son Reuben's school papers in the Hall Collection that show regular school attendance and a bright mind, but

Reuben had been ill from birth following seizures; pictures show an unnatural stance and the journal chronicles frequent illnesses. This project might have been devised to provide entertainment for him in its construction and for visual pleasure in his times of illness. Eleven months after the Locust Box was made, Reuben died of "dropsy" before his tenth birthday. This Locust Box was found in a chest in the attic at the Shunpike Farm along with Reuben's last shoes and small toys—all now in the Hall Family Collection.

It's probable then that during the election of 1860 when Abraham Lincoln, Hannibal Hamlin and the others noted in this box were being elected, that Benjamin thought to keep some of the voting information. Little slips of paper are interspersed throughout his journals that list the local candidates. He might particularly have kept papers about Lincoln's election if the insects had been collected by then, and this plan for a display might already have been forming in his mind waiting for the right time.

His interest in the world of nature and its mysteries, as evidenced in things he has left for posterity, would have helped him form this idea. He also mentions going to Lafayetteville on Fridays to "get the papers," as well as keeping a lifetime of *Herald Tribune Almanacs*, that show his high interest in being knowledgeable about life. Among his things, were several large books in which he had pasted over all the pages with news clippings about world events, science, stories and especially little riddles or jokes. There were no T.V.s then, and these books when full must have provided hours of entertainment. The Hall Family Collection includes his reading glasses.

Figure 5. The Locust Box by Benjamin Hall (close-up view showing political ads in newspapers). March, 1861. Wood, glass, insect carcasses, and newspaper advertisements for political races in 1860. Collection of the Dutchess County Historical Society, the Hall Family Collection. Photograph by Bill Jeffway.

With his higher education, his weekly newspaper reading and saving clippings, and his subscription to the almanac, it is possible he might have read about collecting and mounting insects. However, he took it to a higher, artistic level. A look at vintage insect collections on Ebay shows nothing even close to the manner these insects were displayed. A review of the history of Entomology, the study of insects, though, shows that the serious classification of insects began in the early Victorian period of the 1800s and that this was a time of interest in insect collections. With Benjamin's wide reading habits, he was likely exposed to this new enthusiasm about the insect world, and the 17-year locust with its concern to farmers, would have been the special point of interest to him.

He only mentions making the box once, so it may have been done in one day. His journal reveals also that only chores of necessity would have been done on Sunday. On this particular Sunday, he did not attend Church. He does not say if they were ill as on Sunday, March 3, he notes, "Had the toothache" and there is no usual mention of church attendance. Perhaps the roads were too muddy for getting to the Stanfordville Christian Church. He had noted in the previous week of a S.E. rain storm and a N. E. snow storm. He only notes on the 17ththat it was "cold:" Perhaps it was a good day for an indoor project that was not farm work.

Why was Abraham Lincoln Memorialized in the Box?

But why does Lincoln get involved here? Benjamin, as were farmers generally—in the North, that is—was a Republican. When he went to vote in 1888 he noted,

> Went with Preston to election-to Millbrook. It was the pleasantest election day I have any recollection of, which I think is favorable to republican success in N.Y state as the bulk of the republican party live in the country and stormy weather is more of a hindrance to travel than in the large cities where the bulk of the democratic party reside.

His journal notes regular attendance at political meetings and regular voting. He participated in local politics regularly and held positions as Road Assayer, and School Board member at times. He sometimes noted the ballot counts on the little ballot or candidate lists found in his journal.Over the years his journal shows an interest in national politics as well as local politics. At the time of making the box, Lincoln had not been assassinated, and his assassination in 1865 was never mentioned. He does, however, make note of the assassination of Garfield in 1881 and having seen and heard McKinley speak in 1892.

After seeing how he pasted news clippings in books (one, an old law book), it's easier to see why he would paste in this box, various bits of political news. It might have been his way of dating the box. Notice, that he puts together the information from separate bits of paper—a thoughtful symmetrical balance to the lines. There are six separate bits of paper and different fonts (not noted here) used to present:

REPUBLICAN
ELECTED

Nov. 6, 1860

FOR PRESIDENT
ABRAHAM LINCOLN

FOR VICE PRESIDENT
HANNIBAL HAMLIN

FOR REPRESENTATIVE IN CONGRESS
STEPHEN BAKER

So the stage is set when he found a day just before the end of winter and before the rigors of farm life would begin again, to put together these things he kept. How did Benjamin make and fill the box?

The Construction of the Locust Box

The box is simple. There are two squares of wood, apparently hand-carved, forming the top and bottom. A single hole was drilled in each corner of the top piece, and two holes in each corner of the bottom piece. Hand drills can be seen on Vintage Tool websites. The four pieces of glass—rectangular in shape—were prepared. It looks as if Hall prepared slots in the upper and lower boards for the glass pieces to nest. Since this is a home project by a man known to have been careful with his money and to have had many skills, he probably knew how to cut glass to the size desired. Wires were run through the holes at the top and down through one hole in the bottom and up through the nearby hole. A wire went up the other piece of glass and out the same hole at the top. The two ends were twisted at the top. Done at each corner, these held the glass pieces in place.

Before this assembly however, farmer Hall would have drilled small incomplete holes into the "ceiling" piece and base and arranged the twigs. The insect-shed skins of the larvae and remains of the adults were fixed to the twigs or on leaves in natural positions. The paper clippings with names and dates of political candidates of the fall 1860 election might have been placed first as they are in a symmetrical order and all readable in spite of the seemingly more natural arrangement of twigs.

Some research into the adhesives used in this decade, and the decades prior to the mass manufacturing of glues and availability of plastics, PVA and other resin glues, indicate that adhesives could be made from or mixed from items like milk, cheese, egg whites, beeswax, fish skin and bones, horse parts—horse hooves being the best-known. Milk-based glues were not invented until the 1930s and other synthetic glues in the 1940s. Prior to 1930, most glues were animal based, for example from horse collagen or fish. The first U.S. Patent for glue was issued in 1876, although the first British patent for glue was issued in 1750. Buying a British glue might have been possible, but it's most likely Hall made his own. He had a few cows for milk products; horses were the vehicles of the day, thus old horses for rendering were plentiful; he'd have had plenty of beeswax from his many hives; and he lived near both local ponds and the Hudson River for access to fish. Whatever his recipe for glue, these insects and the paper glued down are still stuck fast after 158 years.

We don't really know exactly when or how Benjamin Hall came to bring together his interest in nature and in politics, his artistic ability and his general handiness with making things for the farm, but the result was an unusual and lovely mounting of insects in a natural setting observable from all four sides.

We are grateful to Margaret Duff, our author and descendant of Benjamin Hall, for this carefully researched and interesting article. I hope the readers will forgive me for my own speculation which I put forward quite tentatively here at the end of this perceptive essay. I would like to suggest that perhaps the learned and intelligent farmer, Benjamin Hall, found a moment of specialness in the fall of 1860, something he wanted to commemorate. He may have seen this in the conjunction of two events: the emergence of the cicadas and the election of Abraham Lincoln. When the cicadas are on the land, everything as we know it is transformed. The music of their bodies fills the air with thrumming. It is magic. Perhaps Hall saw hope in the election at that same moment in time. —C. Lewis, editor

[1] Benjamin J. Hall, *Farm Journal, Years 1851-1896*, of Benjamin Joseph Hall (1825-1896), May be accessed digitally at www.DCHSNY.org . A copy is available at the Dutchess County Historical Society or the original document at DCHS. Last residence The Shunpike Farm, Shunpike Road, Clinton Corners, NY. Residence at time of Locust Box was a farm with a Bangall, New York address. (The original homestead was near Clinton Corners, on what is now Pumpkin Lane.)

[2] Arthur Evans, *National Geographic Backyard Guide to Insects & Spiders*, p. 97. Donald J. Borror and Richard E. White, *A Field Guide to the Insects of America North of Mexico*, p. 129.

[3] "U. Connecticut on Broods of 17-Year Locusts- (a chart)" Hydroductyon.ceb.uconn.edu.

[4] "Timeline of entomology-prior to 1800, From 1800-1850, From 1850-1900" in En.wikipedia.org . Also Whitney Cranshaw, *Garden Insects of North America*, pp. 10, 434.

[5] Hand drills can be seen on vintage tool websites.

[6] See Gluehistory.com; "The History of Adhesives" at Adhesives.org; and Kidsdiscover.com/teacherresources/history-ofglue.

Let Us Go For an Afternoon Walk Around Hopewell Junction

by Charlotte Dodge (1913-2009)

What follows is a narrative from a person who lived in Hopewell Junction during the early twentieth century, the heyday of the railroads there. The narrative is the transcript of an oral presentation by Charlotte Dodge on March 17, 2001. John Desmond, a volunteer for the Hopewell Junction Depot Museum (and member of the Dutchess County Historical Society Publications Committee), transcribed Ms. Dodge's presentation.

The presentation is her account of life in Hopewell Junction in 1923 when she was ten years old. The account reflects daily life among the steam engines that ran through Hopewell Junction and the shops that surrounded the rail yard. John Desmond, himself a retired English professor, notes that Miss Dodge often switches tenses from past to present and back again as if she is swinging from remembering her past to actually reliving it. These switches are maintained here. Miss Dodge's hand-drawn map of Hopewell Junction in 1923 is presented with her narrative. The map can help the reader follow Dodge's details of her walk around Hopewell Junction

—C. Lewis, editor.

Next to the Stevens family [house on Route 82] was an orchard belonging to our farm which contained a few old apple trees, and those trees produced very early yellow apples. It was such a treat after the winter and summer drought of no fresh apples. These trees were also good for climbing. Beyond the orchard was Coleman's Red Onion Hotel and Bar. "Red" because that was its color; "Onion" I know not why. The hotel burned in later years. The cause unknown, but many fires were caused by cinders flying from the engines. It was a marvel of the times that Mrs. Coleman's diamond ring was found in the ashes.

As we approach the railroad tracks, we are stopped by Mr. Wensle who was the guardian of the tracks. He has come out of his little shed with his paddle with a "stop" sign showing; the opposite side reads "go," which he exhibits when the track is clear.

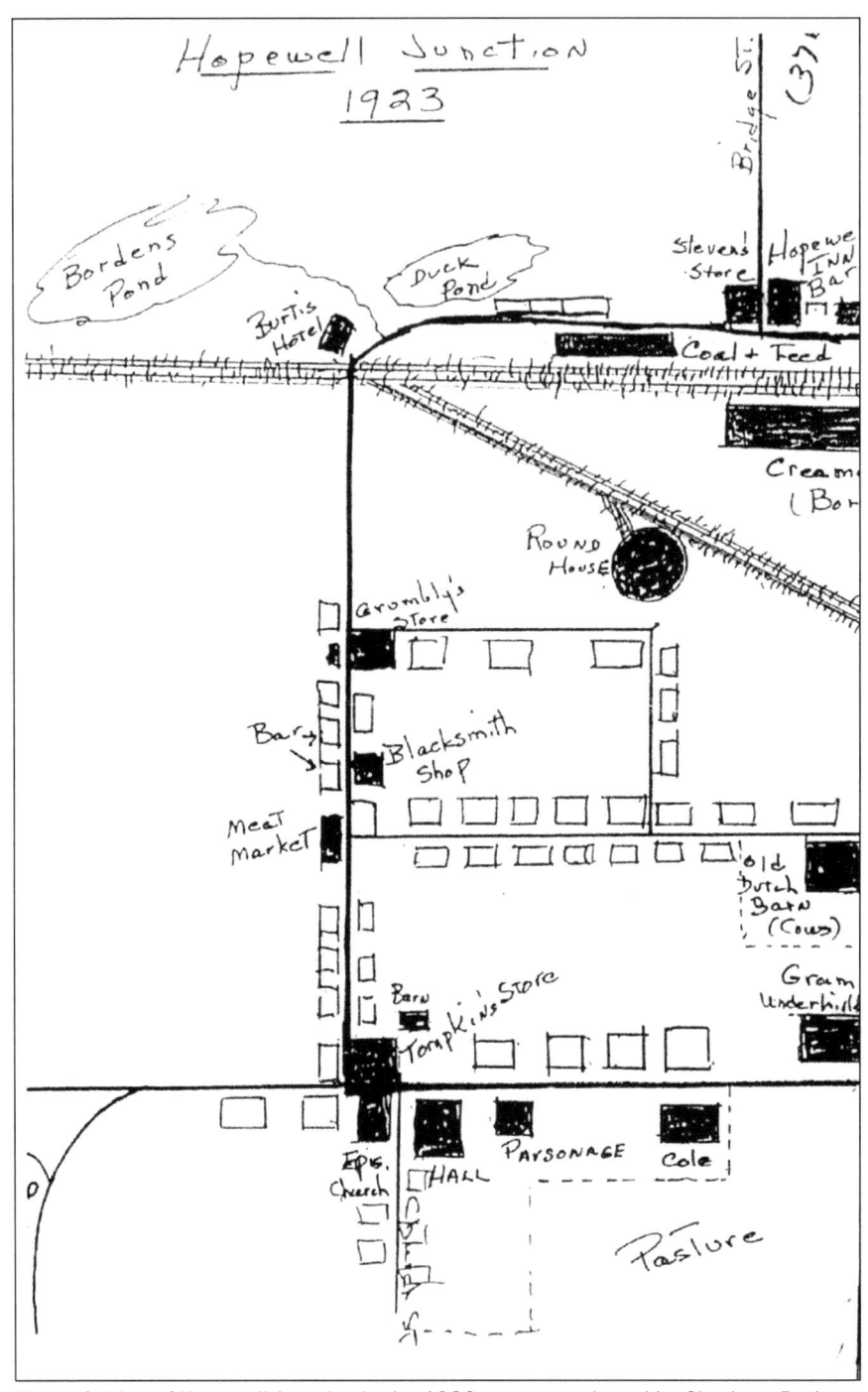

Figure 1. Map of Hopewell Junction in the 1920s as remembered by Charlotte Dodge. Drawn by Miss Dodge.

LET US GO FOR AN AFTERNOON WALK   135

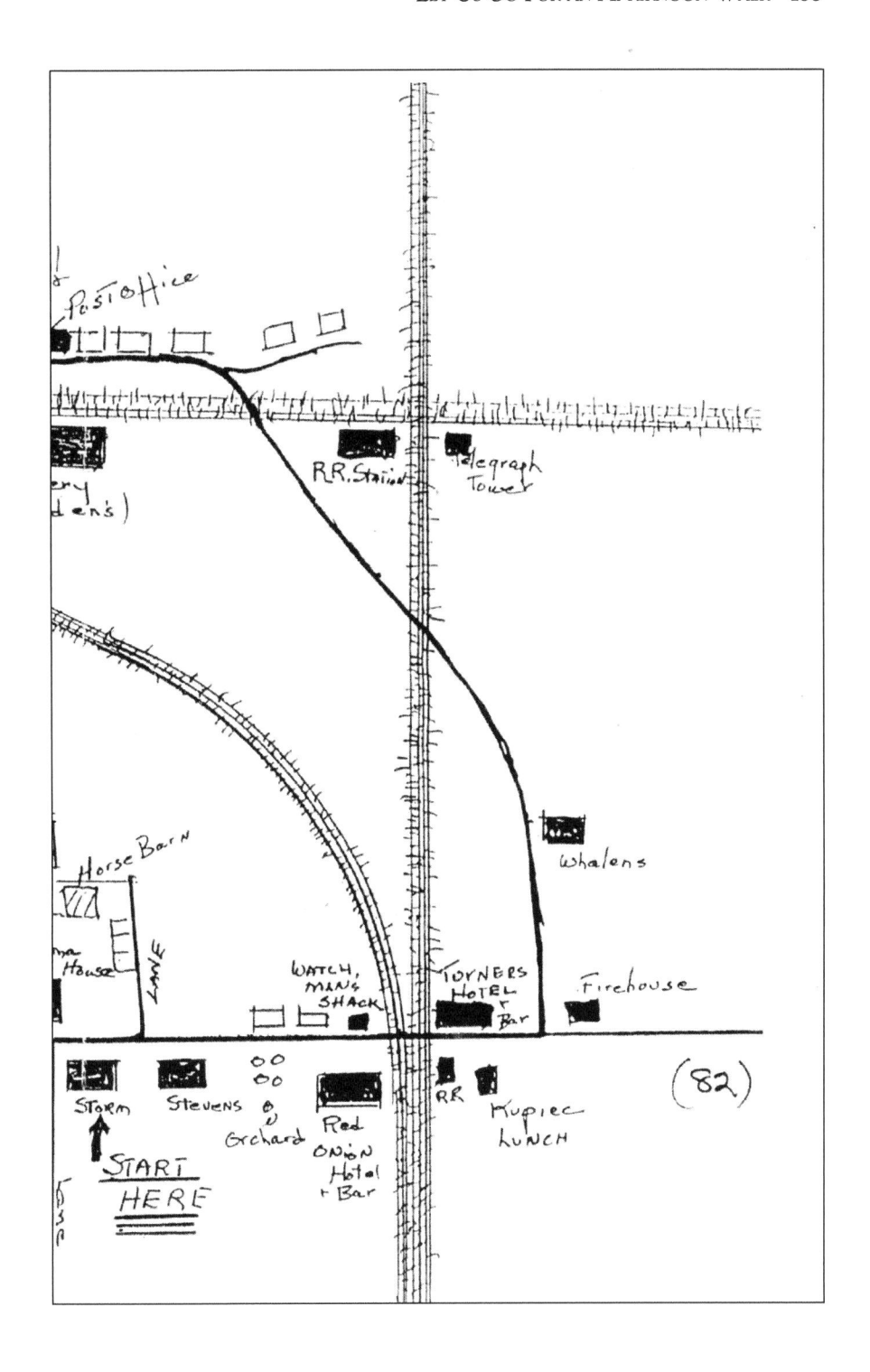

(hand-drawn map with the following labels:)

- Post Office
- R.R. Station
- Telegraph Tower
- Horse Barn
- Lane
- House
- Watch Mans Shack
- Whalens
- Toyners Hotel + Bar
- Firehouse
- Storm
- Stevens
- Red Onion Hotel + Bar
- Orchard
- RR
- Kupiec Lunch
- START HERE
- (82)

Some days we would argue with this man, saying that we can beat that train. Be it known, that if one was held up by one of these trains it could be a lengthy wait because there are many cars on the freights, sometimes numbering over a hundred, with an extra engine in the rear or several engines in the front to help pull or push the cargo over Pawling Mountain.

Today as usual, we wave to the engineer in the engine and again at the flagman in the caboose. We also had to wait for a little handcar which was pumped along the tracks by the workmen who prepared the switches. Safely across the rails, we note a railroad freight building, and next to it is Cupette's lunchroom which we rarely entered. The larger building across the street we gave wide berth to because we might meet up with someone who had been in the bar. It was a hotel run by Mr. Botsinturn, and assisted by his maiden daughter, Annie. Little did we realize that Annie would in World War II keep a jar on the counter urging donations for the soldiers. Not a boy from Hopewell who was in the service failed to receive gifts of cigarettes, candy, and sundries from her.

We now turn to the left, facing as we do the firehouse located in the corner. It has a large iron ring mounted outside, which is struck to announce a fire. The train whistles also blow a special warning perhaps a long and two short toots. To find the exact location of a fire, it was simple to ring Central who was the telephone operator. All of these buildings adjoining the railroad tracks were demolished when the overhead bridge was built, probably in 1935.

We cross more tracks, no watchman here, and come to the station where my Uncle Sam, Marie's father, was the station agent. This station is not bustling today since a passenger train has not long ago left for Poughkeepsie. We snoop around a bit, checking the roll of tickets, the ladies room, and avoiding the spittoons.

Our next stop is the post office, which is a building in a row of houses. It is a pretty active place because everyone in town picks up their mail there. As we enter, we are faced by a wall of boxes. Opening ours, we pick up any mail and proceed on our way.

We note that the Hopewell Inn is flourishing; it is an out-of- bounds place, too. Directly across is Borden's Creamery, where Ruth and Lee have a relative working, so we are welcome there. We encounter the unique odors of warm milk, ice, and sawdust. We are happy to receive a sliver of ice to munch on as we proceed on our way. We stop across the street at Steven's store to pick a loaf of bread my mother has requested. Mr. Stevens is busy filling orders to be delivered and orders he has solicited by personal call on the telephone.

The store is rather dark inside, with an oiled wooden floor and dark walls and counters. No supermarket. There is a lot of merchandise in the store. On one side is the food market: canned goods, eggs, butter, and bread. And on the other side: clothing, including shoes and overshoes, which were called "Arctics", and boots.

Across the road again we go on to check out the feed and coal plant of my grandfather.

He has died the year before, but I can still visualize him, seated at the roll top desk working on accounts, a pipe in his mouth. The bins of feed and seed are fun to run your hands through. Outside is the wooden scale flush with the ground, so wagons and trucks with their loads of coal can pull up and be weighed. It is one of life's marvels to me, since its weight registry is inside the office. I puff up with pride that my grandfather has such a wonderful invention.

Passing the shed and the duck pond, we come to Burtis' Hotel. There is a path between the building and pond which leads to another pond which is the Borden's Creamery [pond] and is used for ice. We never asked for permission to cut through Burtis' yard; it seemed to be a long standing tradition [to cut through the yard]. The same is applied to Bates' yard on Orchard Street. On a sled, we slide under the fence and end up in Whitermen's yard.

Adults were kind and generous to us, and we were pretty well behaved, except, perhaps, on Halloween, when a privy at the school was usually upset. Our good behavior was due in part to everyone knowing who we were, and it being easy to report any misbehavior back to our parents.

Crossing the tracks for the fourth time, we hear no whistle announcing the arrival of a train. The roundhouse is off to the left. We don't usually go in there: the big noisy engines are too intimidating and, perhaps, the busy workmen do not have a welcome mat out for us, as this was the trains' hospital. We do stop at Mr. Grumbly's store, however, where we have the change from the bread to spend. Mr. Grumbly is a bachelor of undisclosed age, somewhat of a recluse. He wears a wig held on by rubber bands. He has an ice-cream fountain in the store with typical ice-cream tables and chairs. He also sells magazines and newspapers, and in front of the store is a wonderful counter with candy. If I had a nickel to spend, it invariably goes for a roll of NECCO wafers. I especially liked the chocolate ones. It would be my turn when one of those appeared. There was also a gasoline tank outside the store, Mary upset it one time, and someone else got it on fire when a lighted match was thrown into a pool of spilled gas. Mr. Grumbly saved his pennies, dumping them in a room upstairs. When he died, there were hundreds of pennies in this room. A barbershop was housed in a rear addition of the store and had its own entrance. Mr. Grumbly also had a grocery store built next door. At the time of our walk it housed the Kings' market, our first chain store. It was followed by the Schaffer store. In 1927, it would be run by Mr. and Mrs. Mc Keel. She is now Wilma Knickerbocker. Her children Louis, Myra, and Ross, all three, are still living in Hopewell.

The tiny building across the way was perhaps a barbershop or maybe a shoe-repair shop. We didn't stop, so I am not sure what was there.

Ahead was one of our favorite shops, the blacksmith run by Mr. Pascoe, George [Bailey's] grandfather. A fascinating place: the stamping of the horses, the switching of the tails, the hot fire pumped by the bellows until it is fiery red, the pounding of the anvil, and the hissing of the hot iron as it is dumped into water for cooling and hardening. And then there is the mystery of nailing the shoe onto the horse's hoof. He didn't even whimper or whine. We didn't bother with the two bars across the street, and we didn't even bother stopping into Dan Lynch's meat market, although he was a very nice man.

It is getting late, and we were due home shortly. Sy Tompkin's store was on the corner. He has a well-known reputation of not being too generous. Wrapping all of his sales in a newspaper, he carried groceries as well as notions, buttons and a bit of yarn goods. I am often asked by my grandmother to run down to the store for some item and am always glad to hear her say keep the change. Sy, too, had a counter of candies.

The Episcopal Church across the street, now Frankie's, is not our church, so we ignore it. Next is Aberdeen Hall. It is owned by the Dutch Reformed Church and is a familiar spot, this being our denomination. There is a supper planned for this night in the basement, which houses the dining room and kitchen. Ladies are bustling around setting the tables. The upstairs of the hall is used for various activities: Sunday-night church services, silent movies with Mr. Mill playing the piano, basketball games, plays, Christmas programs and so forth. When an addition, a long room, stage, and kitchen, was put on the church, Aberdeen was sold to the Catholic Church.

We pass the parsonage, and, as we approached Mrs. Cole's house, her Wednesday-Club friends seem to be leaving. It is often my chore to guide them up the road or to stop the traffic. I leave the girls across from Mrs. Cole's and proceed on home. It is almost time for supper. I hope we will have fried potatoes; I sure do love them.

So this is Hopewell Junction in 1923.

ADDENDA

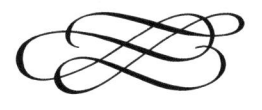

Contributors

John Barry has had a twenty-five-year career as an accountant with a major accounting firm and several years of service in secondary education. Mr. Barry served in the U.S. Marines from 1968 to 1972. After the Vietnam War, he taught at Culver Academy in Indiana. He then shifted his focus to the business world, achieving a Masters in Business Administration from Notre Dame (1977). He worked as a Certified Public Accountant and partner at Coopers & Lybrand in Orlando, Florida from 1977 through 2001. From 2001 through 2014, he returned to education, serving as the CFO of an independent school, a teacher, a coach, and a head of school.

Peter Bedrossian has been a Civil War living historian and re-enactor since 1991. He is currently the military commander of the 150th New York Infantry. If you are a sharp eyed watcher of Civil War themed television and film, you can spot him in the film Gettysburg as well as on the military Channel, the History Channel, and the Smithsonian Channel. His connection to history extends to his professional life and he has been involved with historical interpretation and education for the past fifteen years. He is currently the Program Director at the National Purple Heart Hall of Honor.

John Desmond is a retired professor of English at Dutchess Community College. He co-authored *Adaptation, A Study of Film and Literature*, published by McGraw Hill, in 2005. Since his retirement, he partially occupies his time writing free-lance articles on a number of subjects, from independent-baseball leagues to restored railroad stations.

Charlotte Dodge (1913-2009) was born and raised in Hopewell Junction, in Dutchess County. She later moved with her husband to live in Pennsylvania, but paid frequent visits to her original home. Her account of her youthful memories is included in this issue.

Margaret Duff taught school in Philadelphia for 18 years. Now retired and living in Beaver Falls, PA, she is interested in researching her various family trees. This interest started in the 1960s when she found a farm journal (covering the years 1852-1896) of her great-grandfather Benjamin Hall of Dutchess County. Her mother was a Hall and her mother's ancestors were four generations of Halls who farmed in Dutchess County in the Stanfordville area. Peggy Duff has generously donated the farm journal and other materials from the family collection to the Dutchess County Historical Society to form the Benjamin Hall Collection. She has also written stories for her children and grandchildren based on the family collection of letters and other documents.

Bill Jeffway is the Executive Director of the Dutchess County Historical Society. His first foray into local history involved his joining the Historical Society of his hometown, Northampton, Massachusetts, at age 13. He earned a BA in American Studies and English from Weslyan University before embarking on a 30-year career at the advertising agency, Ogivly & Mather. He worked in their New York, London, Singapore and Los Angeles offices developing communications for American Express, IBM and Cisco Systems.

Bill is a former Trustee of the Putnam (County) History Museum and currently a Board Member of Historic Red Hook. He holds a town council position in Milan, NY, where he had prior served as municipal historian. His book, "This Place Called Milan," marks the town's bicentennial.

He seeks to broaden community interest in local history, especially through digital communications. He founded an advisory group called, "History Speaks," which as the name implies, promotes understanding and appreciation of local history through innovative research and communications.

Candace J. Lewis, Ph.D., is an art historian with a specialty in the field of early Chinese art and a secondary area of interest in nineteenth-century art in America and Europe. She has taught at Vassar College and Marist College. A long-time member of the Dutchess County Historical Society, she became a trustee in 2008, president of the board in 2010, and is now serving as editor of the yearbook. She has lived in Poughkeepsie with her husband, attorney Lou Lewis, since 1969.

Melodye Moore is head of the Collections Committee of the Dutchess County Historical Society and serves as a Trustee on the Board. She is a past recipient of the Helen Wilkinson Reynolds Award from the society. From 1979 to 1986, Moore served as director of DCHS, before taking on the job of managing all site operations at the Staatsburgh State Historic Site (Mills Mansion). Since her retirement from directing the Mills Mansion, she has returned to DCHS as a trustee in 2011.

Elizabeth C. Strauss. In 1976, Elizabeth and her husband, Julian Strauss, returned to Julian's childhood home in Amenia, where he established a veterinary practice and endeavored to maintain the family farm. Elizabeth worked part time at several schools in the area, before taking on the education of her son and daughter at home.

Elizabeth developed an interest in local history, as she became curious about the early settlers of their neighborhood. She was especially interested in the Garnseys (Guernseys), who established their farm in 1759 and lived on the land for seven generations. Elizabeth has continued to research hundreds of the early families of Amenia and North East.

Elizabeth is presently serving on the Amenia and North East Historical Society boards of trustees. She enjoys doing genealogical and historical research on behalf of these societies. Since 2006, she has developed programs and made several presentations for both Amenia and North East historical societies. Elizabeth is also a board member of the Dutchess County Historical Society. In 2018, she was awarded the Helen Wilkinson Reynolds Award for in depth historical research.

Julian Strauss is a retired veterinarian who lives in the town of North East on the farm where he first arrived as a newborn child to his immigrant parents soon after their arrival from Europe in 1935. The Great Depression and WWII are vivid in his childhood memories. Travel and professional work have provided experiences in diverse cultures worldwide, but the farm in Dutchess County has always been his home. He has written one book *A Year in the Life , The 1915 Daily journal of Edward Dean, An Amenia Union Farmer* (2009). His current interest in agricultural history is examining how the love of place has been affected by tumultuous events in a rapidly changing world, and he is writing a book on the topic.

William Tatum III, Ph.D. has held the office of Dutchess County Historian since October 2012. He earned his B.A. in History and Anthropology from the College of William & Mary in Virginia in 2003, his M.A. in History from Brown University in 2004, and his Ph.D., also from Brown University, in 2016. His main area of research is Colonial North America under English rule. In addition to his scholarship, Tatum has been involved in historic site and museum programs throughout the east coast and England.

Dutchess County Historical Society

*Board of Trustees, Advisory Board,
Annual Awards Dinner Committee, Staff*

Board of Trustees 2019

Lou Lewis, Esq., *President*
Christine Altavilla, *Vice President*
Jack Cina, *Treasurer*
Christine Crawford-Oppenheimer, *Secretary*
Michael Boden, Ph.D., Rob Doyle, Eileen Hayden,
Tom Lawrence, Candace Lewis, Ph.D.,
Antonia Mauro, James Nelson, Esq., Melodye Moore,
Elizabeth Strauss, Janna Whearty, Elizabeth Wolf, Esq.
Ex-officio: William P. Tatum III, Ph.D.

Advisory Board

Steven Effron, Brad Kendall, Steve Lant, James Merrell, Ph.D.,
Dennis Murray, Ph.D., Albert Rosenblatt, Esq.,
Julia C. Rosenblatt, Ph.D., Fred Schaeffer, Esq., Paul Sparrow, Ph.D.,
Denise Doring VanBuren, Mary Kay Vrba

Awards Dinner Committee

Lou and Candace Lewis, *Chairmen*
Janna Whearty, Christine Altavilla,
Antonia Mauro, Bill Jeffway

Staff

Bill Jeffway, *Executive Director* • Lainie Lobus, *Bookkeeper*
Shannon Butler, *Collections Archivist* • Adam Raskin, *Research Assistant*

Assisting the Staff: Carol Doran

P.O. Box 88
Poughkeepsie, NY 12602
Location: Clinton House
549 Main Street, Poughkeepsie, NY 12602
845-471-1630
Email: contact@dchsny.org • DCHSNY.org

Dutchess County Historical Society Vice Presidents Representing the Cities and Towns of the County

In 2018, we put in place the full restoration of the long-held tradition of having "local" Vice Presidents who act in a non-executive capacity. They are a single point of contact for the cities, towns, and villages across the county. They might address county-wide issues such as determining how best to obtain and share stories of our veterans. Or they might address a unique or one-off need. Franklin D. Roosevelt served as DCHS Vice President for Hyde Park from 1926 until his death.

Amenia: Julian Strauss
Beacon: Theresa Kraft
Beekman: *Vacant*
Clinton: Craig Marshall
Dover: Caroline Reichenberg and Valerie Larobardier
East Fishkill: Rick Soedler
Fishkill: Joey Cavaccini
Hyde Park: Shannon Butler
Lagrange: *Vacant*
Milan: Victoria LoBrutto
Washington & Millbrook: Jim Inglis
North East & Millerton: Ed Downey & Jane Rossman
Pawling: *Vacant*
Pine Plains: Dyan Wapnick
Pleasant Valley: Dieter Friedrichsen
Poughkeepsie: *Vacant*
Red Hook: Emily Majer
Rhinebeck Town & Village: Michael Frazier & David Miller
Stanford: Kathy Spiers
Union Vale: Fran Wallin
Wappingers: Joey Cavaccini

Directory of Dutchess County Municipal Historians and Historical Societies

Prepared by William P. Tatum III, Ph.D.

Updated July 19, 2019
To update this directory, contact County Historian Will Tatum below.

DUTCHESS COUNTY HISTORIAN
William P. Tatum III
22 Market Street, Poughkeepsie, New York 12601
(845) 486-2381   fax (845) 486-2138
wtatum@dutchessny.gov

DUTCHESS COUNTY HISTORICAL SOCIETY
Bill Jeffway, *Executive Director*
Post Office Box 88, Poughkeepsie, New York 12602
(845) 471-1630
bill.jeffway@dchsny.org

CITY HISTORIANS / HISTORICAL SOCIETIES

Beacon Post Office Box 89, Beacon, New York 12508
Historian: Robert Murphy beaconhistorical@gmail.com
Tel: (845) 831-1514
Historical Society: Diane Lapis dlapis@beaconhistorical.org
beaconhistorical.org (845) 831-0514

Poughkeepsie 62 Civic Center Plaza, Poughkeepsie, New York 12601
Historian: George Lukacs saltglazed@aol.com (845) 471-5066

TOWN & VILLAGE HISTORIANS / HISTORICAL SOCIETIES

Amenia Amenia Town Hall, 4988 Route 22, Amenia, New York 12501
   Historian: *Vacant*
   Historical Society: Betsy Strauss strausshouse72@gmail.com
   Post Office Box 22, Amenia, New York 12501

Beekman 4 Main Street, Poughquag, New York 12570
   Historian: Patricia Goewey
   Tel: (845) 724-5300

Clinton 820 Fiddlers Bridge Road, Rhinebeck, New York 12572
   Historian: Craig Marshall craigmarshall266@aol.com
   (845) 242-5879
   Historical Society: Cynthia Koch cynthiakoch@optonline.net
   clintonhistoricalsociety.org
   Post Office Box 122, Clinton Corners, New York 12514

Dover 126 East Duncan Hill Road, Dover Plains, New York 12522
   Historian: Valerie Larobardier valarobardier@gmail.com
   (845) 849-6025
   Historian: Caroline Reichenberg sweetcaroliner@aol.com
   Historical Society: Fran Braley alfranb@optonline.net
   (845) 832-7949
   180 Old State Route 22, Dover Plains NY 12522

East Fishkill Post Office Box 245, Hopewell Junction, New York 12533
   Historian: David Koehler healthyharvestcsa@gmail.com
   (845) 226-8877
   Historical Society: Rick Soedler rjsoedler@gmail.com
   (845) 227-5374

Fishkill (Town) Fishkill Town Hall, 807 NY Route 52, Fishkill, NY 12524
   Historian: Joseph D. Cavaccini jcavaccini@fishkill-ny.gov
   (845) 831-7800 Ext. 3507
   Historical Society: Steve Lynch asklynch@yahoo.com
   (914) 525-7667
   Post Office Box 133, Fishkill, New York 12524

Fishkill (Village) 40 Broad Street, Fishkill, New York 12524
   Historian: Allan Way allanway2@aol.com

Hyde Park 4383 Albany Post Road, Hyde Park, New York 12538
   Historian: Shannon Butler rangerbutler.sb@gmail.com
   Historical Society: Patsy Costello patsyc97@aol.com (845) 229-2559
   Post Office Box 182, Hyde Park, New York 12538

LaGrange Post Office Box 112, LaGrangeville, New York 12540
   Historian: Georgia Trott-Herring herringtrott@aol.com
   (845) 452-2911
   Historical Society: Bob D'Amato
   lagrangehistoricalsociety@gmail.com (845) 489-5183

Milan Milan Town Hall, 20 Wilcox Circle, Milan, New York 12571
Historian: Vicky LoBrutto victorialobrutto@gmail.com

Millbrook (Village) Washington (Town)
Historian: David Greenwood ngreenwd@aol.com (845) 677-5767
3248 Sharon Turnpike, Millbrook, New York 12545
Historical Society: Dianne McNeill damcneil816@msn.com
Post Office Box 135, Millbrook, New York 12545

Millerton / Northeast
Historian (Town): Lisa Cope northeasttown@taconic.net
(518) 789-3300 ext 603
PO Box 516, Millerton, NY 12546
Historical Society: Ed Downey eddowney@millertonlawyer.com
(518) 789-4442
Post Office Box 727, Millerton, New York 12546

Pawling (Historical Society of Quaker Hill and Pawling)
Historian (Town): Robert Reilly sc31redsky@gmail.com
(845) 855-5040
160 Charles Colman Blvd, Pawling, New York 12564
Historian (Village): *Vacant*
Historical Society: John Brockway johnbetsyb@aol.com
(845) 855-5395
Post Office Box 99, Pawling, New York 12564

Pine Plains
Historian: *Vacant*
Historical Society: Dyan Wapnick dyan.wapnick@gmail.com
(518) 398-5344
Post Office Box 243, Pine Plains, New York 12567
Dutchess County Historical Society VP: Dyan Wapnick
dyan.wapnick@gmail.com

Pleasant Valley
Historian: Fred Schaeffer fredinhv@aol.com (845) 454-1190
1544 Main Street (Route 44), Pleasant Valley, New York 12569
Historical Society: Mary Ellen Cowles merc@hvc.rr.com
DCHS VP: Marilyn Bradford momof5ny@yahoo.com
(845) 518-0998

Poughkeepsie (Town)
Historian: John R. Pinna townhistorian@townofpoughkeepsie-ny.gov
(845) 485-3646
1 Overrocker Road, Poughkeepsie, New York 12603

Red Hook
Historian (Town): Emily Majer emily.majer@gmail.com
7340 South Broadway, Red Hook, New York 12571
Historian (Village): Sally Dwyer-McNulty
sally.dwyer-mcnulty@marist.edu
7467 South Broadway, Red Hook, New York 12571
Historical Society: Claudine Klose claudineklose@gmail.com
(845) 758-1920
Post Office Box 397, Red Hook, New York 12571

Rhinebeck
Historian (Town): Nancy Kelly kinship@hvc.rr.com (845) 876-4592
Historian (Village): Michael Frazier michaelfrazier@earthlink.net
(845) 876-7462
Historical Society: David Miller dhmny@aol.com (845) 750-4486
Post Office Box 291, Rhinebeck, New York 12572

Stanford
Historian: *Vacant*
Historical Society: Kathy Spiers lakeendinn@aol.com (845) 868-7320
Post Office Box 552, Bangall, New York 12506

Tivoli
Historian: Gregory B. Moynahan, Ph.D. moynahan@bard.edu
Post Office Box 5000, Annandale-on-Hudson, New York 12504-5000

Unionvale
Historian: Fran Wallin franw821@hotmail.com
Town Office (845) 724-5600
249 Duncan Road, Lagrangeville, New York 12540
Historical Society: Peter Gay (Vice President) chargaysgy@gmail.com
(845)-677-4837

Wappinger/Wappingers Falls
Town Historian: Joey Cavacinni jcavaccini@townofwappinger.us
Town Office (845) 297-4158 ext 107
Town Hall: 20 Middle Bush Road, Wappingers Falls, NY 12590
Village Co-Historian: Brenda VonBurg (845) 297-2697
Historical Society: Beth Devine info@wappingershistorialsociety.org
(845) 430-9520
Post Office Box 174, Wappinger Falls, New York 12590
wappingershistorialsociety.org

Dutchess County Bar Association
100 years
1919-2019

Row one, left to right: A.B. Smith, Charles Wheaton, William Eno, Seward Barculo, John P.H. Tallman, Allard Anthony, E. Q. Eldridge, Henry D. Varick, Jacob B. Jewett, Henry H. Hustis, Stephen Eno, Edgar Thorn, William I. Thorn, James H. Weeks, Row two, left to right: Ambrose Wager, Walter Farrington, Horace D. Hufcut, Henry M. Taylor, Daniel W. Guernsey, J.S. VanCleef, John Hackett, Robert F. Wilkinson, S.G. Guernsey, Henry E. Losey, Milton A. Fowler, L.B. Sackett, John Rowley, Row three, left to right: O.D.M. Baker, J.V. Doty, Robert Sanford, James C. McCarty, Jacob W. Elseffer, Frank B. Lown, Joseph F. Barnard, Allison Butts, Frank Hasbrouck, Martin Heermance, John H. Millard, William L. DeLacey, Lewis Baker, Row four, left to right: Gilbert Dean, George H. Williams, George Esselstyn, Frank S. Ormsbee, J.L. Williams, S.K. Philips, C.W.H. Arnold, George Card, Henry G. Wolcott, John Thompson, Row five, left to right: Homer A. Nelson, John M. Townsend, Frank G. Rikert, Charles A. Hopkins, George Wood, C.P. Dorland, S.H. Brown, C.E. McCarty, Frank Eno, Edward Crummey, Row Six, left to right: Edmund Phillips, Gaius C. Bolin, Fred E. Ackerman, E.E. Perkins, George Worrall, Benjamin M. Fowler, J. Morchauser, Irving Elting, Safford A. Crummey, A.Lee Wager, Casper L. Odell, J. Hervey Cook, Gerome Williams, Row seven, left to right: Peter Dorlans, Sherwood Phillips, George V.L. Spratt, Leonard Mattice, Charles F. Cossum, John F. Ringwood, H.C. Barker, Henry H. VanCleef, John R. Keech, John H. Elseffer, Walter C. Hull, Isaac S. Wheaton, Charles B. Herrick, Row Eight, left to right: Ransom Baker, William Martin Watson, Jas. S. Dwight, John E. Mack, James E. Carroll, Fred S. Lyke, Joseph A. Daughton, W. E. Hoysradt, Frank J. Connolly, George Overocker, John T. Nevins, Charles M. Smalley, Alexander Down, Cyrus Swan

Dutchess County Bar Association Presidents

1919-1927
Frank B. Lown*

1928
Frank Hasbrouck*

1929
Frederick Barnard*

1930
George Overocker*

1931
John J. Mylod*

1932
C.W.H. Arnold*

1933
Ralph A. Butts*

1934
Elijah T. Russell*

1935
Charles A. Hopkins*

1936
Joseph A. Daughton*

1937
Harry C. Barker*

1938
Edward C. Conger*

1939
John B. Grubb*

1940
Raymond G. Guernsey*

1941
Everett H. Travis*

1941
James E. Carroll*

154 DCHS Yearbook 2019

1942
J. Gordon Flannery*

1943
John R. Schwartz*

1944
Charles J. Corbally*

1945
Gaius C. Bolin, Sr.*

1946
Leonard J. Supple*

1947
William A. Mulvey*

1948
Robert W. Doughty*

1949
Archibald R. Mackennan*

1950
Alexander C. Dow*

1951
John B. VanDeWater*

1952
William B. Duggan*

1953
Joseph A. McCabe*

1954
Benson R. Frost, Sr.*

1955
David G. McCullough*

1956
Earl Hawley*

1957
Charles O'Donnell*

DUTCHESS COUNTY BAR ASSOCIATION 100 YEARS 155

1958
Arthur S. Halpin*

1959
James T. Aspbury*

1960
Frederick W. Heaney*

1961
Lloyd L. Rosenthal

1962
R. Donald Slee*

1963
Ely L. Gellert*

1964
W. Vincent Grady*

1965
Nathaniel Rubin*

1966
John A. Reed*

1967
John J. Mulvey

1968
Charles A. Butts

1969
Edward Kovacs*

1970
John Palisi*

1971
Joseph H. Gellert*

1972
William J. Walsh

1973
Robert J. Marvin

1974
Joseph C. McCabe*

1975
Herman A. Levine

1976
Peter C. McGinnis

1977
Milton M. Haven

1978
John B. Garrity

1979
Edward Rosen

1980
Harold L. Mangold

1981
John A. Wolf

1982
Charlotte M. Frank

1983
Arthur L. Gellert

1984
Robert L. Ostertag

1985
Jack Economou

1986
Damian J. Amodeo

1987
Jennifer L. VanTuyl

1988
J. Joseph McGowan

1989
John K. Gifford

* deceased

DUTCHESS COUNTY BAR ASSOCIATION 100 YEARS 157

1990 Paul Banner, Esq.
1991 Hon. George Marlow
1992 Lou Lewis, Esq.
1993 Paul Goldstein, Esq.
1994 Chester Gordon, Esq.
1995 Frank Redl, Esq.
1996 Donald Brown, Esq.
1997 Jessica Vinall, Esq.
1998 Michael Kranis, Esq.
1999 Fred Schaeffer, Esq.
2000 John Basso, Esq.
2001 Hon. Maria Rosa
2002 Lance Portman, Esq.
2003 Hon. Christine Sproat
2004 Marty Rutberg, Esq.
2005 Kyle Barnett, Esq.
2006 Bryan Schneider, Esq.
2007 G. Brian Morgan, Esq.
2008 Richard Fiorile, Esq.
2009 Maura Barrett, Esq.
2010 Hon. Peter Forman
2011 Rebecca Valk, Esq.
2012 Daniel McCabe, Esq.
2013 Hon. Jonah Triebwasser
2014 Hon. Frank Mora
2015 Sharon Faulkner, Esq.
2016 Kelly Traver, Esq.
2017 Jeffrey Battistoni, Esq.
2018 Veronica McMillan, Esq.
2019 Rachel Hannagan Frost, Esq.

DCHS Donors
Supporters September 2018 to September 2019

$1,000 & Over

Anonymous, Community Foundations of the Hudson Valley

Absolute Auctions & Realty, Inc.

Doris Adams

Central Hudson Gas & Electric,

Cogent Communications

D'Arcangelo & Co., LLP

Dennis & David Dengel

Denise Lawlor Fund

Frank Doherty

Rob & Susan Doyle

John Dyson

Gene Fleishman & Judith Elkin

Julius & Carla Gude

Shirley Handel

Ronald Huber

Lillian Cumming Fund, Rhode Island Community Foundation

Lou & Candace Lewis

Robert & Patricia McAlpine

Melodye Moore & Lenny Miller

N&S Supply of Fishkill, Inc.

National Society Daughters of the American Revolution

James & Margaret Nelson

Poughkeepsie Public Library District

John & Sandra Rankin

Zimmer Brothers Jewelers

$100 to $999

Wint & Tracy Aldrich
Christine Altavilla
Artline Wholesalers, Inc.
John & Anne Atherton
Ronald R. & Elizabeth Atkins
Babiarz Court Reporting Service, Inc.
Harry Baldwin
Paola Bari
Reid Bielenberg
Richard Birch
Joan & Charles Blanksteen
Susan Blodgett
Michael Boden
Darrelyn Brennan
Joseph & Patricia Broun
Peter Bunten
Claramarie Cannon
Paul Cantor
Joan Carter
Martin & Eleanor Charwat
Patricia Corrigan
Christine Crawford-Oppenheimer
Dennis & Susan Creegan
Nic L Inn
John Desmond
Edward & Margaretta Downey
Margaret Duff
Dutchess Community College Assoc., Inc.
Dutchess County Republican Committee
Dutchess County Tourism
EFCO Products
Jack & Rita Effron
Michael Elkin
Nancy Fogel
Peter & Anne Forman
Foster's Coach House Tavern
Joanna Frang & Mark Diebold
Arthur Gellert
Nancy & Mark Giordano
John & Gloria Golden
Jack & Fredrica Goodman
Michael & Deborah Gordon
Robert Gosselink
Nancy Greer
Lee Grotyohann
Handel Foundation
Shirley Handel
Eileen Hayden
Julia Hotton
E. Stuart & Linda Hubbard
Jane Whitman
Brad & Barbara Kendall
Betsy Kopstein Stuts
Virginia LaFalce
Peter & Diane Lapis
Geraldine Laybourne
Edwin Leonard
Lewis & Greer, P.C.
Real Property Abstract & Title Service, LLC
Roderick Link
Victoria Lobrutto
Maryann Lohrey
Stephen Lumb
Cora Mallory-Davis
Marist College
Marshall & Sterling Services Inc.

Craig Marshall
Antonia L. Mauro
Gail & Thomas McGlinchey
Joseph McGowan
Donald & Vera McIntosh
James & Linda Merrell
Kirk Moldoff & Holly Ferris
Kathleen Moyer
Sandra Opdycke
Paul Quartararo, ESQ., PLLC
Peter Jung Fine Art
Philip Peters
Eileen & Denny Quinn
John & Sandra Rankin
Caroline Reichenberg
William Rhoads
Susanne Rittenberry
Riverside Bank
Diane & Randy Rogers
Albert & Julia Rosenblatt
Nancy Rubsam
Susan Serino
Calvin & Diane Smith
Elizabeth Smith
Joan Smith

Kathleen Smith & Christian Rohrbach
Neville & Karen Smythe
Warren Becket Soule
Werner Steger
Sheldon Stowe
Richard Strain
Julian & Betsy Strauss
Mark Tallardy
William Taylor & Jean Anderson
The Exchange Club of Southern Dutchess
Van DeWater & Van DeWater, LLP
Denise Doring VanBuren
Phillip K. & Barbara L. Van Itallie
Carol Vinall
Mary Kay Vrba
Mary Westermann
Stacy Whittaker
Frederick & Sharon Wilhelm
Elizabeth Wolf
Elizabeth Mylod Wolf
Michael Yonchenko
Louis Zuccarello

Under $100

American Antiqarian Society
Damian & Carol Amodeo
Virginia Augerson
Stuart Baker
Leslie Battistoni
Peter Bedrossian
Maria Bell
Carlyle Black

Mary Brockway
Kathleen Brommer
Sara Brower
J. Vincent Buck
Joey Cavaccini
Ellen Chase
John Conklin
Sally & Thomas Cross

James Curatolo
Steven D'Alesio
Daughters of Colonial Wars in the State of New York, Inc,
Dutchess County Dept. of Motor Vehicles
Dutchess County Town Clerks Association
Chez and Roseanne Di Gregorio
Melissa Dietz
Doris Sieck Dubac
John & Abby Dux
Amy R. & Steven L. Effron
Andrew & Barbara Effron
Walter Effron
Kelly Ellenwood
Debra & Robert Erickson
Nancy Ferris
Stephen Fiore
Edwin Fitchett
Gail Fitzpatrick Fox
Wallin France
Michael & Cecily Frazier
Russ Frehling & Debra Blalock
Dieter Friedrichsen
John Gavin
Barbara Geldof
Brian Gerber
Barry & Roni Gurland
Sarah Hermans
John Hicks
Victor & Patricia Hilts
Timothy P. Holls
Judith Hunter
Daniel & Anita Jones
Martin Kline

Claudine K. & Christoper Klose
Theresa Kraft
Shannon LaFrance
Valerie LaRobardier
The Rev. Canon James Elliott Lindsley
Kay Mackey
Lawrence Magill
Mahwenawasigh Chapter NSDAR
Stephen Mazoh
Robert McHugh
Melinda Miller
Arline Minsky
Judith Moran
George Mudge
North East Historical Society
Wendy Palmer
Ann Perry
Philip Peters
Tynan Peterson
Judith Phillips
Jill Potter
Marilyn Pukmel
Suzanne Quigley
Viggo Rambusch
Benjamin Roosa
Robert & Florence Rosen
Melvin & Judith Rullman
Steve & Linda Saland
Sandra C. Strid
J. David Schmidt
Winifred Schulman
David Schwartz
Janice Selage
Celia and Arnold Serotsky
Alice Sheppard

Ann Shershin
Marguerite Spratt
Anne Strain
James Taylor
Elfriede Tillman
Town of Dover Lions Club
Mary Tuohy
Jacques Van Zyl

Nancy VanCoughnett
Richard & Ellen Wager
Ann Wentworth
Richard Wiedeman
William P. Tatum III
Michael Williams
Matthew Winchester
Andrew Zobler & Manny Arquiza

Lifetime Members

Herman Harmelink
Homeland Foundation
Michael Levin
Lou & Candace Lewis
Zinas Mavadones
W.P. McDermott
Melodye Moore & Lenny Miller
Harold Nestler

Sheila Newman
Joan Sherman
Paul South
Norma Shirley
C. B. Spross
Peter & Myna VanKleeck
William Wade

The Society encourages the use of memorial donations to remember a loved one, or the gift of a special donation in honor of one's birthday, anniversary, or special occasion. Please be assured that all such remembrances will be appropriately acknowledged with a special letter from the Society expressing our sincerest thanks.

It has been the policy of the Dutchess County Historical Society to print only the categories seen above due to space limitations. We certainly value all of our member and donors, including Lifetime, Individual, Family, and Organization. We appreciate each and every one of you. Thank you for your continued support as we move forward into our second one hundred years.